WRITING AND ILLUSTRATING CHILDREN'S BOOKS

for

PUBLICATION

Two Perspectives

by Berthe Amoss and Eric Suben

This hardcover edition of Writing and Illustrating Children's Books for Publication features a "self jacket" that eliminates the need for a separate dust jacket. It provides sturdy protection for your book while it saves paper, trees and energy.

The authors and publisher have made every effort to trace the ownership of all copyrighted material reproduced in this book. They now acknowledge and thank the following individuals and entities for permission to use such material:

Mike Artell
Atlantic-Little Brown
Matt Berman
Rebecca Blake
Andrea Cascardi
Jean Cassells
Cynthia G. Dike
Emma D. Dryden
Chuck Galey
Aimee Garn
Joan Elizabeth Goodman
Carrel Muller Gueringer
Harcourt Brace and Company
HarperCollins Publishers
Kenny Harrison
Susan Larson
Lerner Publications
Emily Arnold McCully
Diane Muldrow
Meb Norton
Oxford University Press
Auseklis Ozols
Richard Peck
Patsy H. Perritt
Random House, Inc.
Jennifer Rosen
Amye Rosenberg
Coleen Salley
Scholastic, Inc.
Whitney Stewart
The New Yorker Magazine, Inc.
The Times-Picayune
The Word Among Us
UFS, Inc.
Walker & Co.
Jennifer Weltz
Beth Woods

Any use of copyrighted material without permission is the result of inadvertence or mistake and will be corrected in future printings after written notice to the publisher.

Edited by Alice Pope
Written by Berthe Amoss and Eric Suben
Interior design by Rebecca Blake
Cover design by Rebecca Blake
Cover illustrations by Berthe Amoss

Table of Contents

INTRODUCTION

"I wish we had included that in *Writing and Illustrating*!" How many times we have said this over the last ten years referring to some event, such as the advent of Harry Potter, that has changed the children's-book scene dramatically.

"I know so much more about that now with ten years more experience in teaching, writing, and illustrating." Another oft-repeated phrase by one of us.

And so it was with great enthusiasm that we accepted the Writer's Digest request to update our book for a tenth anniversary edition. "At least 30 per cent new material," they told us. Our editor, Alice Pope, was much more explicit, going over our book page by page with suggestions as to how to make *Writing and Illustrating* more meaningful to you, our readers.

We are pleased to offer you the tenth anniversary edition of *Writing and Illustrating Children's Books for Publication*, still *Two Perspectives*, the book's unique voice that speaks from both sides of the desk, the author/illustrator's side and that of the editor/publisher, still filled with even more fascinating case histories and success stories, which we have always thought the most effective way to teach.

The most important remaining element in our book that we hope will be apparent is our love for what we do and our desire to share it with you. Use *Writing and Illustrating* as a self-taught course or as a reference book for your career in the children's-book field. Good luck and happy writing and illustrating.

— *Berthe Amoss & Eric Suben*

Berthe (pronounced bear-t) is the author/illustrator of numerous picture books and four young-adult novels. She taught children's literature at Tulane University for 14 years and also wrote a column on children's books for The Times-Picayune *during that time. With her husband and their six sons, she lived and studied art in Germany, Belgium, and Hawaii. She and her husband now live in New Orleans and in Pass Christian, Mississippi.*

Eric was formerly editor-in-chief of Golden Books and is the author of more than 40 picture books for children. He was a director of the Children's Book Council and has been a frequent panelist and lecturer on children's publishing. Presently an attorney with a major entertainment company, Eric is also on the faculty of the prestigious Gotham Writers' Workshop in New York City, where he lives with his wife and children.

Berthe & Eric met at a local SCBWI meeting just as Eric began studying law at Tulane. They have been giving workshops on how to write and illustrate children's books ever since.

Chapter 1

PROMISES

---

*I*f you want to write for children, your biggest problem may be finding time. You have a demanding job in an office or small children at home or both of the above and then some. Perhaps you're not sure you have talent or if your idea is right or if you should do your own illustrations.

Maybe you've already written something and want to get it published but don't know how to go about it. Should you get an agent, and if so, how? You've heard of books that were accepted "over the transom," as the saying goes; will someone read your manuscript if you just mail it to a publisher? And what about mailing it to more than one publisher at a time?

And then, there's the greatest mystery of all: What are editors looking for? Ursula Nordstrom of Harper & Row, one of the most influential editors of children's books in our times, answered that question: "I don't know," she said, "but I recognize it when I see it."

This is our promise to you: If you read this book, using it to guide you as you write your own book for children, you will be able to produce a publishable manuscript, and you will understand the process of getting it published.

We believe this book is different from, and more helpful than, any other you may have read on the subject of writing and illustrating children's books. We believe this because of two unique concepts incorporated in the format:

I am Sophie, the Tenth Muse. My nine sisters and I inspire and guide mortals in the arts. My field is Children's Literature. Do not mistake me for an angel because of the wings. They are Monarch butterfly wings, functional for getting around and symbolic of the miraculous transformation (caterpillar to butterfly) I can achieve in my followers: from eager, searching creators or users of children's books to confident, skilled professionals.

I am not a cute gimmick invented by Berthe and Eric because they have run out of ideas. I am as real as the child within or the right side of the brain. I was born in 1928, when Wanda Gàg published *Millions of Cats*, the first true picture book, and have been around all that time. Eric and Berthe have given me graphic form because I know new ways to do things and I tell it like it is in children's literature.

Our book gives you two perspectives, that of the editor and that of the creator, and it uses the case-history method to convey the information you need in order to be successful.

Two Perspectives is designed so that it can be used in different ways. There are ten chapters, eight of which have the following features: Advice, Case Histories, Exercises, Reading Lists, and Self-Editing Checklists. For easy reference, each part can be identified by its own logo, which symbolizes the "the inner child" or Sophie, the Tenth Muse.

ADVICE

This section of each chapter will explain as clearly as possible the main areas of concern and opportunities for development under each subject heading. Where possible, we attempt to give concrete examples and use graphic devices, such as charts, to impart information in a lucid, memorable way. The Advice sections of this book draw heavily from work with students and from our teaching experience.

CASE HISTORIES

The case histories are stories from our own actual experiences and from working with other authors, illustrators, and editors. Generally, the stories are dramatic illustrations of the points discussed in the text. Sometimes, however, a case history will show an instance where an exception to one of our "rules" was the right approach, and sometimes a case history will be included for the fun of showing the wacky things that happen in publishing. Because these stories are truly products of our different perspectives, we have identified some with the name of whichever of us supplied the incident.

WRITING AND ILLUSTRATING EXERCISES

The exercises are included to help you build important skills discussed in the text. Doing the exercises should help you focus on the process of writing for children by concentrating your mind on the challenges and helping you build techniques for overcoming them. Sometimes we do not give an answer to an exercise because the goal is for you to find your own answer and in this way become more flexible in identifying different approaches to your writing and illustrating. The exercises are designed to further your own story and to keep you writing every day, another important aspect of creating a successful book for children. The assignments pull together the threads developed by the chapter's exercises, and each is designed to have a practical result, such as writing down an idea, or writing a query letter, or making a book dummy or outline or doing your own illustrations.

READING LISTS

Reading is one of the most important things you can do if you want to write well. The lists have been prepared carefully with the help of teachers, booksellers, and librarians who know children and their literature. Listed are children's books as well as books written for adults with a strong interest in writing for children.

SELF-EDITING CHECKLISTS

These lists of questions and reminders provide guidelines for assessing the work you've done in your own story. The lists will help you polish your work so that it is as good as can be before you submit it to an editor. You will be able to view your work critically and anticipate what an editor would find wrong in your story.

Because an illustrator is involved, your work may not be finished until the book is on the press. The collaborative publishing process requires that you be flexible, cooperative, and willing to solve problems. Most important and often overlooked is the need to spell and use grammar correctly. Look for redundancies and gaps in logic, and fix them before an editor must. Submitting a clean, well-written, carefully edited manuscript gives you a far better chance of being read by a busy editor, who might be turned off by time-consuming sloppiness, no matter how much talent is hidden in the pages.

You can use *Two Perspectives* in different ways, depending on your personal goals. It can be used as a reference book, and you can dip into it as the need arises. We have also designed the book as an eight-lesson, self-taught course. Using this approach, the reader works through each chapter in order, doing the exercises, answering the questions, reading the suggested books, and working on his own story as he goes along.

By using the book in this manner, the reader can produce a publishable picture book manuscript in eight weeks, that is, one chapter per week. If you are writing a chapter book, you should be able to finish three polished chapters and an outline. You can, of course, extend the time spent on each of our eight "course" chapters, but we recommend as short a period as possible. Long-term commitments are difficult for most people, and we believe that it is crucial to complete a manuscript and actually send it off to a publisher.

If you take the course approach, you will find that the lessons work all together. (Chapters one and ten are intended to provoke your thinking and are not directed at building skills as the other eight chapters are.) As you grow more confident in your skills, you may do things in a different order or spend more time on one lesson. For now, separating the skills you need into discrete challenges is an organized way to learn and grow.

We can give you the tools to succeed, but you must learn to use them; the commitment and hard work must come from you.

"Yes, but what I really want to do is write children's books."

The Fundamentals: Two R's and Two W's

There are some constants, things you should do continuously as you work your way through this book.

1) Read

Spend time in bookstores and libraries. Go through your children's or any children's bookshelves. Constant exposure to the vast range of material published for children can help you appreciate the wide variety of opportunities and possibilities in writing for children. It can also help you learn what is considered publishable.

Poking through bookstores doesn't require a great investment of money: Picture books are short, and you can read several while you stand casually browsing through the children's shelves. The advantage to reading in a bookstore is that you can watch the reactions that children and parents have to books. Talk to the bookseller; most will be happy to share their observations with you. You can hear something about the reasons parents buy particular books. And you can see how books are merchandised, formatted, illustrated, positioned on shelves or in displays, hand sold by bookstore personnel.

Many children's books are sold because booksellers take time to "push" them to consumers. Listen to what booksellers say in recommending books. Ask them which books are selling best and why, which are their favorites and why. Remember that after you sell your book to a publisher, the publisher sells it to a bookseller. The bookseller is the first "consumer" of your book. If she doesn't like it, it will never get on the shelves and have the opportunity to appeal to parents and children. (On the other hand, remember, too, that one bookseller's opinion is only one bookseller's opinion.)

Follow the same line of questioning with children's librarians. Remember that their tastes tend to be more conservative — they're looking for redeeming value, not just fun, but they are the tastemakers in the field of children's books, the reviewers and award-givers. Traditionally, they also comprise one of the largest and most lucrative markets for children's books.

At the library, request and read the children's-book reviews in *Publishers Weekly*, *School Library Journal*, *Voice of Youth Advocates*, *Horn Book*, and other publications. You'll find reviews of children's books in your local newspaper as well. Comb the reviews for glimmerings of ideas that you might like to handle. Find the books and read them. Try to find what the reviewer liked or didn't like about the book. Figure out how the author or illustrator did it.

2) Remember

Think back to your own childhood, to the stories and books you liked best, the questions you wondered about most, the people, places, things, and experiences you liked best and least, and why. Think of situations you were in that revealed something about your inner thoughts and feelings, even though you may not have been aware of them at the time.

Remember that a tiny event from your childhood may have seemed like a great dramatic episode to you, and it may contain the germ of an idea to start you on a story. Your memory should become your greatest source of inspiration, not only for story ideas, but also for true feelings to express in your writing. Think about what happened to you at different times, but also about how it made you feel. Try to remember your interests at different ages. Try to remember what you were doing at the time of those different experiences: Could you swim? Could you read? Could you ride a trike? A bike? Could you tie your own shoes? Remembering surrounding circumstances can help make the experience truthful in your writing. Try to picture the scenes you remember, and write down the details.

3) WATCH

Observe children at every opportunity — on city buses, at playgrounds, at parties. Be aware of their ages and the interests and skills they have developed. What are their motor skills?

If you hear them say things that intrigue you, take notes and look for germs of ideas. If you have or know school-age children, talk to teachers. What curriculum is your child learning this year? What skills does the teacher expect the children to master? Think of ways to work these concepts into stories — letters, numbers, colors, opposites, word recognition, addition and subtraction. What books does the teacher read to her classes? What is the classroom setting like? Are the children responsible for plants? Animals? What is the classroom routine?

If you have not watched children for a while, make the effort to observe them for what they wear, say, do. Watch children's television and movies. They can help you understand children's interests. They can instruct you in ways of expressing meaningful themes through colorful characters and action. Look for high-quality media presentations. The people at Pixar, Disney, and Nickelodeon know a great deal about educating, entertaining, and enriching children. You can learn a lot from their work.

Watch the world around you. What did you always want to know about that a child might like to know about, too? Why do animals do the things they do? Why is the sky blue?

In our workshops, we have noticed that participants who are around children (teachers, librarians, mothers) often begin with a very definite idea for a book based on a need they perceive. For example, the mother of a handicapped child might want to write a book that explains her child's handicap to other children so that her child will find acceptance and understanding among peers.

Or a librarian might want to write a book about a subject that he perceives is missing from library shelves but requested by children. Beverly Cleary, a librarian, wrote her classic *Ramona* because children kept asking for books about other children like themselves. Cleary's editor said, "I never edit Beverly's books; I only rearrange commas." Librarians know what children like, and they know how to write.

4) WRITE

The most important thing you can do is write. Keep a journal, and if you are writing a picture book, illustrate your journal with your own drawings. Even if you are not working on a story, write down your opinions of the books you read. Take notes on the children you watch. Put your memories into words. Writing is like any other skill, requiring constant exercise to improve. When you are not working on a manuscript, keep a written record of your thoughts, feelings, and observations that apply to children and children's books.

If you are working on a manuscript, do some writing on it every day — even a sentence or two can be constructive. The most important thing you can do in working on a story is to keep the ball rolling, to stay in the world of your story with the characters you've created. You may find a new and better way to express your ideas, a more accurate or appropriate description. A story is a living, growing thing: You are bringing the characters and situation to life through your words. Like other living things, your story requires attention and care. Take time to nurture it with new writing every day.

You may reach a point where you are frustrated with your story or have created a problem you don't know how to solve. Put it aside temporarily and start on something new. By facing a new set of challenges, you may find a way out of your problem in the first story while you are creating another manuscript. A dividend of this style of working may be that you end up with two good stories to sell rather than one. Although your aim should always be quality rather than quantity, remember that the more stories you write, the more opportunities you give yourself to be published.

In your writing, even in the journal you keep for yourself, be conscious of writing in the simplest, most direct language. Keep a dictionary and thesaurus close at hand, and make sure you are using and spelling any questionable words correctly. Keep a style guide, such as Strunk & White's *The Elements of Style*, at hand, and check your punctuation, capitalization, and usage. Words and punctuation are your tools, and you should be sure you are using them correctly. If you are, editors will love you, because you are saving them work.

Periodically read through your journal for thoughts or ideas you may have overlooked in thinking about stories to write. Go back to unfinished stories and try to finish them. Do not throw away any drafts or early stages of your manuscripts — as you write and revise, you may want to refer to them. Read your writing aloud. Read it to others whose opinion you trust, and listen to their criticism.

Our success is based primarily on luck and perseverance. We do believe that we have talent, but we also believe that if you yearn to write for children, you also have talent. The word *yearn* is the essence of talent. We believe that if you're persistent enough, the law of averages almost always catches up with you and you will get published. Feel the passion, have faith, and do the hard work. We've put our "two perspective" tools for your success into this book; it is our kept promise to you.

Chapter 2

THE CHILD WITHIN

IDEAS AND GETTING STARTED

*Y*ou may be reading this book with the idea that when you finish, you will begin to write your own book. If that is what you're doing, you've already put a "writer's block" in the middle of your path to success.

To take full advantage of *Two Perspectives*, you should make up your mind that you are going to write a book as you read and that when you have completed the book, you will have a finished manuscript. If you already have a finished manuscript, you should work on it as you progress through the book.

Reading about writing but not actually writing on a regular basis gives you only the illusion of learning. Our advice to you (and we will say it over and over again because it is the most important thing of all) is this: Form the habit of writing every day, whether it is work on your manuscript or journal-keeping.

This chapter is devoted to helping you organize and get started. The best way to do this is to find your special time and place, and set a goal. Plan to have a finished manuscript at the end of eight weeks.

But first, let us define clearly the categories of children's books in use throughout.

We can divide children's books into categories by age group, by subject matter, by genre, etc. But categories often overlap, and reading levels aren't always consistent with age levels. Also, the most successful books (e.g., E. B. White's *Charlotte's Web*) defy labels and are just plain good literature.

For the purposes of this book, however, we will define the three broad categories we refer to most often:

- PICTURE BOOK: a book for very young children in which the illustrations play a role as important as the text; for children approximately two to six.

- CHAPTER BOOK: a longer book for older children who are learning or have just learned to read, with more sophisticated subject matter, treatment, and language; for children approximately six to ten.

- YOUNG ADULT (YA) NOVEL: within the novel category are two distinct subcategories, one for ten- to 12-year-olds and another for ages 12 and older which contains more mature subject matter and language suitable for young teens.

If you're writing a short picture book, eight weeks is long enough to make a "dummy," a handmade book with sketches, to submit to a publisher. If you're writing a chapter book or a YA, you can complete three polished chapters and an outline. Knowing that you will have a completed project at the end of eight weeks will motivate you to make a time commitment and postpone things that aren't absolutely necessary.

To help you find time, think of it this way: There are some things you must continue to do, but if you think about it, you will find that

FINDING TIME (BERTHE)

When my children were small, I got up at five every morning to write my first young adult novel, *The Chalk Cross*. It was the only time of the day I could call my own, and I grew to love that special time with my characters, so much so that I still keep to my schedule. When I am all alone in the early morning, I really feel as though I have entered another world, the world of my characters.

For me, there is something almost magic about the place I choose to do my work. It is a small room upstairs lined with books. It has a large casement window and a battered, upholstered chair, my girlhood desk, and my drawing table. Early in the morning, when I come into my room, once occupied by a small son, I open the window to a still-dark sky, and enter my fictional world.

The Chalk Cross was set in 1840 in New Orleans, and I had to do a lot of research. I read in snatches of time, e.g., when the children napped or at play time while I sat with them. When I had to do finished watercolor illustrations for my first picture book, I hired a baby-sitter for three hours every afternoon.

Writing *Lost Magic*, set in medieval times, required even more research, but by the time I wrote it, my children were older and I could spend hours at the library or growing and studying medieval herb gardens, even visiting herb gardens in England, Connecticut, and the Cloisters in New York.

you are currently doing a lot of things that aren't really necessary; if you postpone or eliminate these things for just eight weeks, you can find two hours a day for your writing. If you're a night person, stay up after your house is quiet. If you think better in the morning, wake up early. If you work, use your lunch hour.

Choose a writing place and keep everything you need there, so that you won't waste time looking for a sharpened pencil or having to put paper in the typewriter or printer when you have time to write.

A loose-leaf binder containing everything you need can go with you everywhere. Use indexed sections to organize and separate various parts or chapters of your writing, envelope dividers for material relating to your subject, and one plastic page with a zipper for pencils and a pencil sharpener.

Carry your binder in your briefcase if you go to work, or keep it at your writing place at home so that you can pick it up quickly if you have a moment and can't get to a word processor. Just eight weeks, remember!

Think one chapter at a time and a novel does not

ONLY CONNECT (BERTHE)

When I went back to school for my master's degree in English and art, I connected each of my courses with children's literature. In creative writing, a short story became a chapter in a young adult novel, and in art history, I studied Wanda Gàg, a printmaker of the 1920s and the author/illustrator of the classic *Millions of Cats*.

DO YOUR HOMEWORK (BERTHE)

Back in the sixties, after four years of rejections, it dawned on me that I couldn't write. My illustrations intrigued editors, but my stories turned them off. I looked around for a course on how to write children's books and finally found one, a university correspondence course. My assignments forced me to write and read a lot of children's books. I remember one enlightening assignment: two children are going on a picnic and are disappointed by rain. Write this as a story for children four to six years old and then write it for those six to eight years old. That exercise helped me a lot.

Because of all the reading and writing I was doing for this course, I was so immersed in children's literature that I began thinking and dreaming in the form of children's books. Then, when my nine-year-old son had a birthday and my three-year-old a temper tantrum, I "recognized" my story and wrote *It's Not Your Birthday* before Tom's last howl had faded. I knew when I wrote that story that it "worked," as they love to say in publishing, and six weeks later Ursula Nordstrom of Harper & Row accepted it.

I still have some of my earlier, failed attempts at producing a picture book, and I can't believe I didn't see at the time why they were not accepted for publication. What is obvious to me now I have learned from experience. The more you read and write, the more you'll be able to see your own work as an editor might.

seem such a formidable task. It is said that Margaret Mitchell used that approach when she wrote *Gone With the Wind*, stacking each completed chapter in a pile behind her desk.

"Only connect" is a phrase out of E.M. Forster's *Howards End*. It was used also by P.L. Travers, author of *Mary Poppins*, as her title for an essay on children's literature. Take it for your mantra, and connect everything you do so that all your activities relate to your writing.

By making everything you have to do relate to what you are writing and/or illustrating, you're really doing two things at once: saving time and creating an environment for developing ideas. You may think that your "real" job is totally unrelated to writing children's books, but that's only because the idea of connecting is new to you. Try it and you'll see what we mean. "Only connect" is a kind of mind-set.

Finding ideas is easy if you're around children, but if you're not, take comfort from the fact that some of the best writers for children — such as Maurice Sendak, author of the classic *Where the Wild Things Are* — aren't either. Besides that's only one way to get ideas. The real trick is to change the phrase "looking for ideas" to "recognizing ideas," and you'll soon see that good material is all around you. If your mind is set and you are thinking "children's books," everything that happens during the day will suggest ideas to you.

Talent? It's buried in all of us; it just has to be nourished. As we said earlier, we believe that talent is composed of large quantities of yearning, hard work, a strong desire to express yourself in writing or illustration, and a willingness to devote yourself to the task. If you examine the careers of

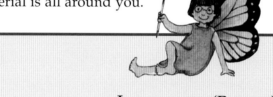

JOURNALING (BERTHE)

My first journals were spiral notebooks with envelopes as dividers. They are a great mishmash of travel diaries, rough drafts of newspaper columns, ideas for writing, sketches, pressed flowers and diarylike observations. I took them everywhere and filled several a year. At one time I had a superstition: If I wrote a story in the back of my notebook starting on the last page and moving forward Japanese-style, my story would be published. It worked, but only at times! Even now, I can find a germ of an idea in old journals. Journaling is a great way to practice writing and nourish those ideas that could vanish if you don't write them down while they're fresh.

published writers, you'll find that hard work, perseverance, and luck played major roles in their success. For now, the most important thing you can do is to get started with a goal in mind.

Read as many children's books as possible. Haunt the children's sections of bookstores and libraries. Talk to librarians and booksellers. Observe children's reactions to their books; they are the final judges of their own literature. No book ever became a classic if children did not love it. Read, write, and think children's books. If you do, you'll "recognize" your idea when you see it, and if you've organized your time, found your special place to work, and set a goal, you will be well on your way to success.

At the start, nothing is more important than remembering what it was like to be a child — not the those-were-the-days kind of remembering, but recapturing how you felt and thought about the world around you, rediscovering the child within. Often that childlike point of view will surprise you because you have replaced it with something more appropriate to maturity. Would-be writers for children who are not in touch with the child within often write little sermons instead of stories; they are writing from an adult point of view, thinking they have to teach or preach to the little ones. Although every good book for children enriches the reader in some way, the message always emerges from the story in the form of its theme, never in a didactic way.

Journal-writing is another way to reach the child within and to begin to see again the world from a child's point of view. An illustrated journal with sketches you've drawn is even better.

Don't say you can't draw. If you have trouble thinking of yourself as an artist, then think of yourself as a reporter and record in picture form what you see or whatever needs illustrating.

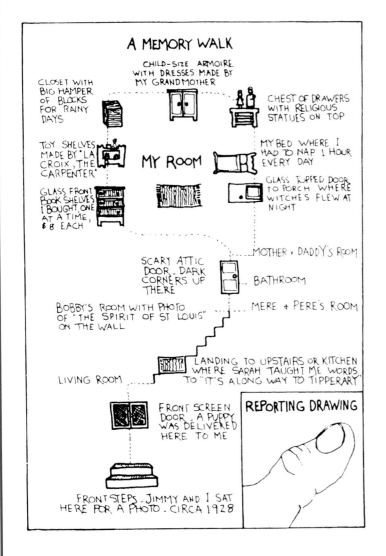

A MEMORY WALK

CLOSET WITH BIG HAMPER OF BLOCKS FOR RAINY DAYS

CHILD-SIZE ARMOIRE WITH DRESSES MADE BY MY GRANDMOTHER

CHEST OF DRAWERS WITH RELIGIOUS STATUES ON TOP

TOY SHELVES MADE BY 'LA CROIX, THE CARPENTER'

MY ROOM

MY BED WHERE I HAD TO NAP 1 HOUR EVERY DAY

GLASS FRONT BOOK SHELVES I BOUGHT ONE AT A TIME, $8 EACH

GLASS TOPPED DOOR TO PORCH WHERE WITCHES FLEW AT NIGHT

MOTHER + DADDY'S ROOM

SCARY ATTIC DOOR. DARK CORNERS UP THERE

BATHROOM

BOBBY'S ROOM WITH PHOTO OF "THE SPIRIT OF ST LOUIS" ON THE WALL

MERE + PERE'S ROOM

LANDING TO UPSTAIRS OR KITCHEN WHERE SARAH TAUGHT ME WORDS TO "IT'S A LONG WAY TO TIPPERARY"

LIVING ROOM

FRONT SCREEN DOOR. A PUPPY WAS DELIVERED HERE TO ME

REPORTING DRAWING

FRONT STEPS. JIMMY AND I SAT HERE FOR A PHOTO. CIRCA 1928

Here is my memory map of my bedroom in the house I lived in until I was 12, more than 50 years ago. Drawing it, I remembered forgotten incidents loaded with emotion and feeling I had then for people and things, a childlike view of the world.

NOTES ON INSPIRATION, NANCY WILLARD

One of the writers we admire most is Nancy Willard. Nancy is a poet who, in her own words, "also writes for children." She wrote *A Visit to William Blake's Inn*, which was the first book of poetry ever to win the prestigious Newbery Medal.

In an interview she told how she came to write *A Visit to William Blake's Inn*. "It helps me to make a model of the thing I am writing about. I suppose the most outrageous example of this is in *A Visit to William Blake's Inn*. Three things came together. An editor asked me to do a collection of poems for children. She said I could do them on anything I wanted.

"I had been hearing a recording of someone reading Blake's poetry, *Songs of Innocence and Experience,* and I had a lot of it in my head. At the same time I was building a house, a very small house — well, not so small, it's six feet tall and it's in the dining room. I like to make things with my hands and I thought I would make a house and all the characters in it and that would be William Blake's Inn! It started out with odds and ends of found materials: broken dishes, jewelry, corks, old ashtrays, just all kinds of odds and ends, things from my scrap basket. The character called the Marmalade Man, a guest of the Inn, started out as a bright orange Burger King eraser, a little man with a crown, I think. He has since gone through many transmutations. That was the Inn. So I was hearing Blake's poems. I soon began to add a tiger and a few other things, and numerous angels, and then the poems began to be about the things that I was making."

Page from SONGS OF INNOCENCE by William Blake.

Cover illustration from A VISIT TO WILLIAM BLAKE'S INN by Nancy Willard, © 1981 by Alice Provensen and Martin Provensen, reproduced by permission of Harcourt, Brace & Company.

Nancy Willard told this story: "There is no good children's book that is only for children. The kind of literature that crosses the boundary most often between adult and children is fantasy, which is really for all ages. One of my favorite books of fantasy is *Alice in Wonderland*. I read it when I was eight and I was much amused to hear a friend say that he had to go into the hospital for an eye operation and was allowed to read for only one hour a day for an extended period of time. What book could he bring that would sustain him? He didn't bring the Bible because I think he already knew it so well. He wanted something that would make him laugh and keep up his interest for that precious hour. He brought *Alice in Wonderland*. You can call it a book for children, but clearly, it's a book for all ages.

"I think that is also true of fairy tales. Fairy tales were originally told by grown-ups to other grown-ups, by women to other women as they sat in their spinning rooms in their houses passing time."

Nancy Willard's latest book is **The Tale of Paradise Lost**, a prose retelling for young people of the poem by John Milton. It is illustrated by Jude Daly, and has already received starred reviews.

EXERCISE

Choose an unlined, spiral drawing tablet or a bound, blank-page book for your illustrated journal. Make sure the paper is of good quality so that you can use both sides, sketch in watercolor, or paste in photos. A cloth-bound blank book may inhibit you with its pristine beauty until you take pencil in hand and fill it up with writing and sketches that make it yours. If you want to make your journal and sketches part of your notebook, add loose-leaf sheets for the journal and another to hold your sketches.

Don't worry if your drawings aren't "good." They will be good for you because they will capture for you the essence of the thing you're thinking of in a way nothing else can.

When you're not working on a manuscript, write and sketch in your illustrated journal. Let it be a continuation of your thinking. Use simple language; the shortest distance between you and the publisher is clean, fresh prose. Study the masters: E.B. White, Beatrix Potter, Mark Twain, and, of course, J.K. Rowling. Use a good dictionary, a thesaurus, and a writing manual. Words and punctuation are tools that can work for or against you; know how to use them.

Don't worry that someone has already used your idea. If you write from the inside out, it will be your story.

"Call me shallow—I like 'Goodnight Moon.' "

WRITING EXERCISE

Nancy Willard also suggested an interesting exercise: "The entire text of *Night Story* [a picture book by Nancy Willard] started out as a poem published in an anthology and someone said it would make a wonderful picture book and set it up that way so each line is a page with a picture. It is a particular form which I think is very useful if you are just starting to write for children and you want to know how to begin. It is in a form called a litany, which gives you enough structure so that you can choose something to get hold of but does not hamper you. It's not rhymed but every line starts with the same word. You hear litanies in church and the psalms are full of poems of that sort. *Goodnight Moon* is written this way. It is a very mysterious form but if you want to write a picture book text, start there because you have so much to go on."

EXERCISE

1) Make a "reporter drawing" describing an object nearby.
2) Do a memory map of a place dear to you in your childhood: your bedroom, backyard, classroom, etc. As you draw, you will remember forgotten events. This is a great way to put you in touch with "the child within."

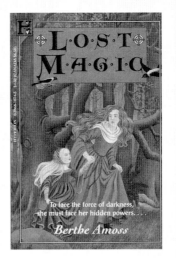

WRITING EXERCISE

I was invited to talk to a school assembly of children from grades one through five. I decided to talk about book jackets and began by showing them Diane Stanley's beautiful jacket for one of my own books, *Lost Magic*, a story set in medieval times. Ceridwen's enemies accuse her of bringing the Black Plague to Bedevere and want to burn her for a witch. Diane Stanley's beautiful jacket shows Ceridwen and Elinor fleeing through the forest.

Now, I said to the assembly, I am working on a sequel. It is about Elinor who is fourteen and an artist; she must marry a gross-looking man twice her age in order to protect her kingdom. It is also about John, a peasant boy of sixteen who yearns to be a knight but is trapped by the feudal system.

I gave the children a form to fill out and sketch in. Here are example of what they did.

What can be learned from these children's responses is that certain subjects are hooks: Children like magic, princesses, knights, jousting; they love action, a good story and mystery. It is a wonderful age to write and illustrate for, less crowded than the picture-book field, and more receptive than children twelve and up who would rather be caught dead than with "a book for young adults."

CHOOSING A TITLE AND COVER ILLUSTRATION
for the sequel to Lost Magic

I. Check the best title:
    (√) Looking for Magic
    (√) Searching for Magic
    (   ) Other:

II. Check the best cover illustration:
    (   ) John, the peasant boy, dressed as a squire with a knight on horseback, about to start the joust.
    (   ) Elinor, as a bride, getting married in the castle chapel.
    (   ) Elinor, in Ceridwen's tower room, painting an herb with a ghost-like Ceridwen looking on.
    (   ) Elinor and John together at the tournament, Elinor watching the joust, John assisting a knight on horseback.
    (√) Other.

III. Sketch chosen illustration:

Progress Checklist

- Get ready to begin by choosing a regular time and place to work.
- Make sure you have pencils and paper, a dictionary, thesaurus, and style guide at your work place.
- Do the exercises in this chapter (start your illustrated journal and do memory walk and reporter drawing).

Reading List

Here's a list of books that formed our tastes and influenced our work. Although it's important to keep up with trends, it is just as important to know what's gone before so that you can build on it.

Goodnight Moon by Margaret Wise Brown

The Little Bookroom by Eleanor Farjeon

Little Tim and the Brave Sea Captain by Edward Ardizzone

The House of Sixty Fathers by Meindert de Jong

Charlotte's Web by E. B. White

The Court of the Stone Children by Eleanor Cameron

The Tombs of Atuan by Ursula K. Le Guin

The Tale of Peter Rabbit by Beatrix Potter

Harold and the Purple Crayon by Crockett Johnson

The Important Book by Margaret Wise Brown

A Hole Is to Dig by Ruth Krauss

Where the Wild Things Are by Maurice Sendak

Pat the Bunny by Dorothy Kunhardt

Noah's Ark by Peter Spier

Millions of Cats by Wanda Gàg

Madeline by Ludwig Bemelmans

Curious George by H. A. Rey

Chapter 3

WHAT IS IT?

FORMAT, THEME, AND AGE LEVEL

*T*here used to be a clear distinction between children's books and adult books — children's books covered a wide range, from board books for the youngest children to novels for teenagers. Then came Harry Potter. Novels for young people, sure. But for the first time, throngs of adults were lining up to read books that were published with young readers in mind. At the upper end of the age range, the line between children's books and adult books is blurred. But there are still some important differences.

Early in the process of writing your story, you will make important decisions about the length, tone, and theme of your book, as well as the need for illustrations and whether your characters will be animal or human. In the first flush of inspiration, your story may flow out in a form that feels "right," and you may not consciously weigh these choices as you make them. Later, you will want to consider the appropriateness of your decisions in the cool light of reason. You will find that the choices you make about format, message, and characters are motivated by one central factor — the age of your intended reader.

Like children, children's books come in many shapes and sizes. Even a subject like dinosaurs, which seems like a standard topic, may lend itself

to different treatments appropriate for different formats and age groups. A book about baby dinosaurs and very small dinosaur species may be ideal for a very small-sized picture book, as well as for a small-sized reader who can relate to the special vulnerability these dinosaurs experienced on account of their diminutive size. If you want to emphasize the monumental scale of the most popular dinosaur species, you may want to visualize a very large book. In this case recognize that you will need to provide enough substance to justify your large-scale treatment.

Picture books depend as much on their illustrations as on their text. That's why, even if you're only going to write, it's important that you have an image in your mind of what the page is going to say. In picture books, the illustrations tell part of the story. Think of it this way: There's a difference between an illustrated book and a picture book. Look at *The Tale of Peter Rabbit* by Beatrix Potter. You could read the text without looking at the pictures and you would not miss any of the story because the illustrations are not interpreting or adding to the plot. Beatrix Potter says nothing in the illustrations that she hasn't already said in the text. *Peter Rabbit* is an illustrated book.

Now look at *Where the Wild Things Are*. Maurice Sendak's pictures are indispensable to an understanding of the plot. In the beginning, Max, the little boy who misbehaves, is described as "making mischief of one kind or another." In the picture, you see that Max is nailing something into the wall and has been cruel to the dog. There are pages without any words at all where the monsters Max creates out of his fantasy grow bigger and more horrible. You can see the monsters

THE WAY IT WAS (BERTHE)

In 1961, I decided I wanted to illustrate children's books. We were living in Europe at the time and were coming home on a freighter to New Orleans for vacation. But I was pregnant with my fifth child and not allowed to travel by ship. I flew via New York, and on the advice of a writer friend, I brought with me a huge portfolio of drawings, the best of what I'd done in art school and some dreadful little stories I'd hastily written to go with illustrations to show an editor. Totally ignorant of the publishing world, I followed my friend's further advice. "Just barge right in," she said, "they're looking for talent." I liked the books Harper & Row published, so I went there. Barging in hardly fits my timid, terrified entrance to Harper's office, but I have been lucky all of my life, and the person who literally opened the door at Harper was a kind, sympathetic young woman who took the time to look at my illustrations and stories. She liked the illustrations and she showed me how to make a book dummy. She told me I would then see how to pace my story and how to balance pictures and words. I know now that if she hadn't taken the trouble to encourage me, I wouldn't have pursued the idea of writing and illustrating children's books. And if I hadn't learned how to make a book dummy, I might never have succeeded in getting any story "right." Susan Hirschman, the young woman who opened the door at Harper's, became one of the most respected editors in children's books as editor-in-chief of Greenwillow Books. She retired in 2003.

dancing at the same time you see Max's expression showing that he's not afraid, he's brave and has it all under control. A lot of content is in the pictures, and writers who are not also illustrators must keep this in mind. *Where the Wild Things Are* is a picture book par excellence.

MAKING A BOOK DUMMY

Remember that each page of your book will have a picture, and for your own sake, make a book dummy. A dummy of a picture book is a handmade book. It can include simple black-and-white line drawings or just verbal descriptions of what the pictures should show. Picture books are sometimes 24 pages long, but more often they contain 32 pages. All page counts in books are usually multiples of 16. Books are printed all on one big sheet of paper; eight pages are printed on one side of the sheet, eight pages on the other. The sheet is then folded and cut. These 16-page groupings, called signatures, are then gathered and bound to form the book. You need to know this information about page counts because you need to plan and present your book in a manner that is realistic from the manufacturing and marketing point of view.

Imagining each page of your book will help you know exactly how much writing you have to do. It can also reassure you that your idea is big enough to make a picture book. Big is a relative term: Something big

MAKING A DUMMY

Use the idea you have selected and begin a book dummy. Count the first five pages as being the title page, copyright page, dedication, etc. This material is known to publishers as frontmatter. Begin your story on the right-hand side, page 5; end it on page 32 on the left-hand side. Take a large sheet of paper and fold it eight times, then tear it so you have 16 pages. Now you can think about your story in discrete events or episodes, one to a page.

doesn't have to happen on every page. Nothing big has to happen from page to page so long as everything that does happen helps communicate a clear, consistent theme. The *theme* is different from the *idea* of your book. Your idea may be to write a book about baby dinosaurs. But your theme will be showing that, though they started out small, these dinosaurs grew big and strong and were soon able to fend for themselves. Think of the theme as the glue that holds your entire book together. Everything that happens must in some way illustrate this basic message, this universal element that children can relate to and take away with them as an opportunity for growth. Don't let your book get didactic, though. Your theme should be illustrated by the events that happen in your book, not prosaically told in so many words. The theme should be below the surface of every event in the story.

What publishers call children's books cover a very wide range of publishing. There are complex fantasies with deep, dark themes, like the *His Dark Materials* trilogy of Philip Pullman. On the other hand, there are very simple books of eight or 12 pages printed on cloth or vinyl. Such books are for the very youngest children and usually are so simple to plan and write that publishers rarely look to outside authors to execute them. This wide range of formats is one of the great opportunities before the children's writer. Because picture books may be convincingly presented in any of a variety of

WRITING WITH A SPECIAL FORMAT IN MIND

The first picture-book we did together was *The Secret of Pirate's Manor*. We had a format with a jigsaw puzzle in the cover. We had a story about a hunt for buried treasure in an old haunted house. How could we use the puzzle format and tell the story so that the two were integrated — in other words, so that solving the puzzle helped solve the mystery of the treasure's whereabouts? Realizing that we could print on both sides of the puzzle, we worked out the story so that the young reader could flip over the pieces and put together the picture showing the climax of the story where the protagonists found the treasure. Thus, the special feature helped entice the reader, set the scene, and solve the mystery all at the same time. It also helped us, as author and illustrator, make the most of the picture-book format by allowing us to "show" in pictures rather than "tell" in words.

shapes and sizes, you can make a distinctive format part of your thinking for your book and part of your presentation to publishers. Picture books can be soft-cover or hardcover; big or little; printed on cardboard or plastic; cut into shapes, or packaged with dolls. Be expansive in your thinking, but make sure the format you have in mind reflects the theme of your book. Special format books are usually for quite young children. You must be sure that your subject matter, your ideal format, and your target reader all work together. A book shaped like a yellow school bus may sound like a fun idea, but do two-year-olds ride a yellow school bus? Format and age group are closely linked. Past age three or four, the standard 32-page picture book will be the norm. The publisher is usually the one to make exotic format choices. However, if you think a special feature or format would strengthen your proposal, go ahead and present your inventive idea to a publisher whose books demonstrate a level of comfort with innovative formats. After all, no one had published a "touch-and-feel" book before Dorothy Kunhardt came to Golden Books with the idea for *Pat the Bunny*. That book was the first of its kind and broke all sales records for children's books.

Planning is equally important if you want to write a chapter book or novel. You will know that this is the proper format if your story concerns children old

FORMATS BY AGE GROUP

Following is a rough grouping of children's book formats listed with the age groups for which they are designed:

six months to two years	cloth books; board books; floating bath books; "touch-and-feel" books; "shape" books
two years to five years	simple picture books; "toy" books with wheels, puzzle pieces, etc.; pop-ups and novelties
five years to seven years	more sophisticated picture books; joke books; various kinds of informational books; simple easy-to-read books
seven years to nine years	more sophisticated informational books; chapter books
nine years to 12 years	middle-grade novels and nonfiction
12 years and up	young adult (YA) novels and nonfiction

enough to read for themselves. Chances are that you cannot write an entire novel in one burst of inspiration, as you sometimes can with a picture book. So instead of making a book dummy or writing out illustration suggestions, you need an outline spelling out chapter-by-chapter what will happen. You need not adhere slavishly to your outline once you get going; let the story move of its own force. A plan at the outset, a goal in sight with several smaller goals along the way, will keep your work in manageable segments so you can reach the great goal of completion.

New writers — and we have seen this often in our workshops — often err in creating elaborate fantasies for publication as picture books. Such stories often take the form of outer-space adventures, or adventures underground or "through the looking glass." Think about the fantasies that have succeeded with young readers, the Harry Potter books, the Philip Pullman series — novels all. A rich, well-defined, meaningful fantasy world is almost impossible to create in the few words and few pages of a children's picture book. By the time you've explained your world and special characters, there's no more room to tell the story. Let yourself relax if your idea is to write such a story; expand your idea along clear, logical lines, and make sure you tell a cogent story. If you're thinking this way, try to cast your work as a novel.

EASY TO READ, HARD TO WRITE (ERIC)

Sometimes your text will not match up with the age of your readers. Recently I wrote my first "easy to read" stories. They were written for a publisher's "hi-lo" program — the subject matter had to have a high interest level among children in the target age group; but the reading level had to be low enough for children reading below grade level. In this case, the target readers were sixth graders reading at a third-grade level. It was tough! I wrote a group of sports stories. The publisher set me up with a computer program that did a readability analysis of each draft. Every time I thought I had told a coherent story as simply as possible, the program would tell me that my text was too difficult by one or two decimal points. I would then tinker until I finally came in under the readability target. If you want to write for the easy-to-read market, you'll find that most publishers have some way to vet the reading level of the work. And reading level derives not only from vocabulary, but from word repetition and sentence length. Easy to read is a rewarding area; but it is hard to write!

CHECKLIST

Ask yourself these questions as you plan your book:

1. When I visualize my book, what do I see?

2. How old are my characters? Are they animals? People?

3. How old are the readers who would be interested in my idea?

4. Are 32 pages too many? Too few?

5. Do I see a picture on every page?

6. Would a special feature — shape, a pop-up, etc. — add something to my idea?

7. If the book I visualize looks like another book, what book is that?

Remember that small children tend to be literal-minded, partly because they don't have a wealth of associations for each new idea that comes along. Don't overwhelm picture-book readers with too much to digest. Visualize your characters and visualize a reader who is like them. Can they read? Can they write? Do they go to school? What grade? Is their focus home, or is it outside the home? Decide what kind of book you're writing by whom you see in your mind's eye.

A REASON TO RHYME (ERIC)

Many children's writers are tempted to write in verse. Most children's-book professionals will tell you that you are better off writing in prose. Verse is technically challenging, and publishers will hold you to the highest standards. Each rhyme must be a "true" rhyme (i.e., no "tree/breeze" or "cough/laugh" pairings), and your meter must be strong and consistent throughout. It is difficult to accomplish these technical goals while expressing your meaning clearly. I was so daunted that after 25 years in the business and with more than 40 books to my credit, I had never attempted to write in verse. However, I recently found myself writing a little story about some fish, and the editor asked me to try it in verse. I ran out and bought a copy of Dr. Seuss' *One Fish, Two Fish, Red Fish, Blue Fish* for inspiration. I found myself with a very tight, difficult meter, and tinkered with each word — even each syllable — to make it work. In the end, I was satisfied: The text was very compressed but fun to say. The editor liked it, too, though he confided that others in his office had differed with a few of my choices. "You know how it is," he told me. "Every editor thinks he's a poetry maven." However, the editorial director was very happy with my work. He had wanted the book in verse so it would be reminiscent of *One Fish, Two Fish*. . . . Without knowing it, I had sought out just the right model!

Don't Stick to an Outline, but Fall Back On One!

There is something very comforting about an outline even if you don't intend to follow it exactly. First of all, it keeps your theme or goal firmly in your mind. You can think of the outline as a journey toward the goal, each chapter a step in that journey that brings you closer to the end. I was so nervous writing my first young adult novel, that I made an outline, or rather two woven together, because it was a time-warp story, part of it taking place in 1840 and the other in the present day. It comforted me to know when I was in one century, I knew where I'd emerge in the next. I worried about the transitions, but I actually enjoyed writing them because I had my outline to fall back on. For the YA I am now writing, the sequel to *Lost Magic*, I have divided a loose-leaf notebook into eleven segments, one for each of ten titled chapters and another for plans, ideas and outline. I do not write chronologically, that is, beginning at chapter one and ending at chapter ten. I think in bits and pieces and put those pieces into my notebook where they fit. This technique works for me and allows my characters the freedom to change the plot. Making an outline for your story and adapting it to your style of writing may mean that you crumple up your outline and throw it in the trash can, but it is worth a try!

Reading List

The books on this list have distinctive formats. As you look at each, try to discern the intended audience for each and note how the format adds something to the book.

In My World by Lois Ehlert

The Rainbow Fish by Marcus Pfister

The Adventures of Captain Underpants by Dav Pilkey

Trucks, Trucks, Trucks by Peter Sís

Blue & Square by Hervé Tullet

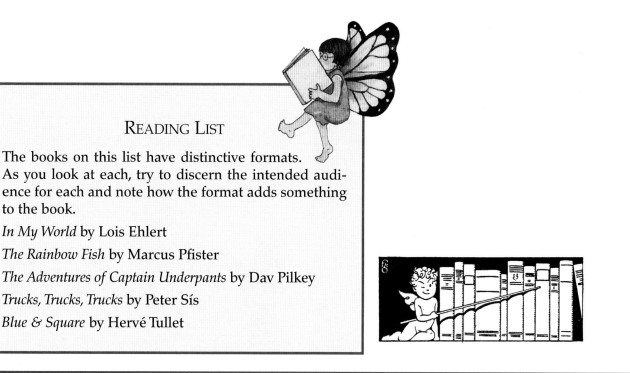

Chapter 4

WHERE, WHO, WHEN?

OR SETTING, CHARACTERS, PLOT

*I*f we could give just one piece of advice, it would be to write about something you care about passionately. Don't be beguiled by what you perceive is a market trend. There may be an explosion of interest in dinosaurs, but if you, the writer, are sick to death of them or were never interested in them to begin with, it will show in your writing and your book will be just another lifeless manuscript sure to be rejected. A strong, personal interest in your subject makes it unique and gives it life.

You can prove this to yourself by writing a paragraph on a current, topical theme you are not terribly keen on. Now write a paragraph on something you care deeply about. Don't reread these paragraphs for at least one hour, preferably one day. When you come back to them you will see how much more vivid and thought-provoking your second paragraph is than your first. You may even surprise yourself and find that your spontaneous writing done from the heart is far better than you believed you could do.

SETTING

The same holds true for time and place. Set your book in a time that interests you, one that you've lived and know — or if it's in the past, one you'd enjoy researching. Even if yours is a picture book for very young children, make sure your setting is one you understand and feel comfortable in from the point of view of the child within.

If you're writing a chapter book or YA novel set in the past, read about your period in history books, newspapers, novels, letters, or diaries written at the time. You'll be able to place your story in an historical context and give it authenticity if you know how the people thought, dressed, and talked. Be aware that the world that surrounded them was so different from ours, with far less information and technology.

Be sure your facts are correct. You will need to do a lot of research if your setting is historical, but if you like the period, research reading is fun, and it often presents you with new ideas to enrich your story. A sense of time and place is essential to your writing. If you, the writer, are comfortable and knowledgeable in a time and place, it will come through in your writing and make it real for the reader.

THE WAY IT WAS (BERTHE)

Ten years ago, I had just completed a picture book, *The Cajun Gingerbread Boy*. I began with a simple retelling of the folk tale and generic landscapes through which the gingerbread boy, a paper doll, runs (the pages are slit). My editor, Liz Gordon, who knows my background, suggested a Cajun retelling with Louisiana landscapes. I groaned and whined, something we strongly recommend against, but the book is now far stronger than my first draft because I know and love its setting. Even so, I spent the summer running around southwest Louisiana with my camera and sketchbook. I visited plantation houses, walked the fields of sugar cane, climbed fences and waded in bayous to bring home water hyacinths for painting. I enjoyed my research until I realized I was using it as an excuse not to face up to that clean, empty watercolor paper. But when I finally glued myself to the drawing board, I was comfortable in the Cajun setting I know and love. Now, thanks to my editor, *The Cajun Gingerbread Boy* has come out in a tenth anniversary edition.

For example, if your story takes place in the tropics, what kinds of flowers and plants might your characters encounter? What moods and colors bring to mind a warm sun, a blue sky, a soft breeze? What about the smell of jasmine? Suntan oil? A well-known author wrote about the "sweet scent of azaleas." Azaleas don't have a scent! Be careful. Don't make flowers bloom in the wrong season or give them a fragrance they don't have.

If you are writing fantasy, you still have to abide by the laws your fantasy world dictates. There is no such thing in fantasy as a magic wand to make everything turn out all right just because the world of your book is imaginary. Fantasy requires research, too, best done by reading the classic fairy and folk tales, where you will find there is more reality than fantasy and see that the fantasy must abide by laws sometimes even more rigid than those of reality! Begin with the works of George Macdonald, C.S. Lewis, and J.R.R. Tolkien, and top it off by studying the Harry Potter books. That's difficult to do at first reading because the story is so engrossing, but read those books again and see how J.K. Rowling blends fantasy with reality and makes a school for wizards entirely plausible.

KEEP IT REAL (BERTHE)

Lost Magic is about Ceridwen, a fourteenth-century "herb woman" who inherits magical power from a legendary sorcerer. But Ceridwen cannot use her gift until she develops it very much as a young person must study and hone her talents to achieve her full potential. Being an incurable romantic, I wanted Ceridwen to marry Robert, the handsome Lord of Bedevere, but given the times and Ceridwen's position in life, and in spite of her magical power, it could never have happened without weakening the whole story. Characters are real only when they behave as they would in real life.

LISTENING TO THE YOUNG (BERTHE)

Richard Peck, a former teacher, Newbery Medalist for *A Year Down Yonder*, and author of many YA novels, understands young people. He speaks to them in schools, asks them what matters to them and what they'd like for him to write about. He is not above eavesdropping on young people at their favorite, near-school haunt. Once, I invited him to speak to my students in children's literature at Tulane. I was afraid he might bore those sophisticated young college students and appear too juvenile in his approach. When he was finished, my only fear was that I would not be able to pry him loose from the students who clustered around him, asking questions and revealing their feelings to him. Small wonder Richard Peck's characters speak with authenticity.

Richard Peck's "Grandma," the main character in *A Year Down Yonder*, is probably responsible for garnering that prized Newbery Medal. See page 96 for more about Richard Peck.

If your book has a contemporary setting, your characters must act and think as today's children do. That's not as easy as it sounds. Each generation has a language, even a culture of its own, and whereas human nature doesn't change, customs and mores do. And even if you are a young writer, the manners and customs of a ten-year-old have changed since you were a child.

The best way to understand how children and young people behave and think is to observe them. Teachers, librarians, and parents have a catbird seat, but even if you don't belong to one of those groups, you can still observe children at playgrounds and young people in their local hangouts. Movies give you a good idea of contemporary culture, and you can read books by authors popular with children who write about the way it is today. Observation is all-important, but don't forget what we've said about the child within and remembering how you felt as a child. Although that remains the same and almost universal, the way children act changes each decade if not seasonally, and although you don't have to like the changes, you have to be aware of them to speak to today's young people.

CHARACTERS

Concentrate on your characters. If you can make them believable to yourself, they will be real to your readers. "Real" characters will plot your book for you, almost as though they are telling you their story. This may sound like an exaggeration, but it's true and it works.

How can you create believable characters? The process is somewhat mysterious and varies with different writers. Characters often begin with a real person the writer has in mind and evolve into quite different people.

"Real" characters will never act "out of character." You cannot manipulate them to behave in a certain way if they would not do so in real life. If you have created a shy, introspective boy, he will not campaign for class

---

WRITING EXERCISE

YA: Write a one-page character sketch of each of your characters. This writing will not appear in your story but will help you get to know your characters.

DIALOGUE EXERCISE

Use a situation from your own writing or one of the following:

1. A 13-year-old boy wants to go somewhere and his mother and father don't approve.

2. A six-year-old child is trying to convince his parent that he needs a pet.

3. Write a dialogue between two people. Do not use any "he saids." All of the text must be within the quotation marks. Try to identify the speaker by his own words and show the situation without description.

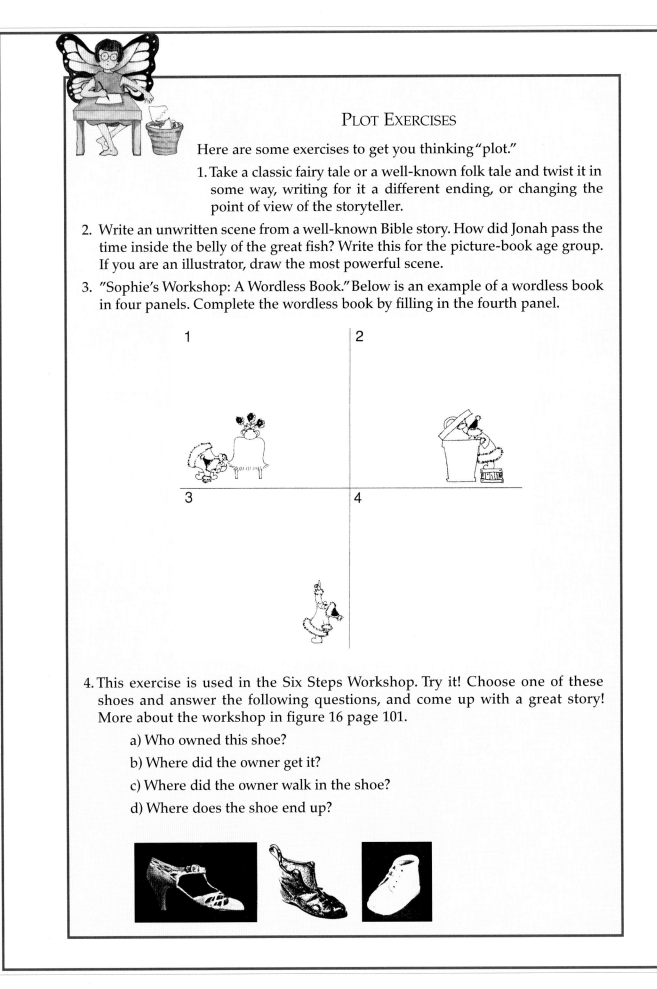

PLOT EXERCISES

Here are some exercises to get you thinking "plot."

1. Take a classic fairy tale or a well-known folk tale and twist it in some way, writing for it a different ending, or changing the point of view of the storyteller.

2. Write an unwritten scene from a well-known Bible story. How did Jonah pass the time inside the belly of the great fish? Write this for the picture-book age group. If you are an illustrator, draw the most powerful scene.

3. "Sophie's Workshop: A Wordless Book." Below is an example of a wordless book in four panels. Complete the wordless book by filling in the fourth panel.

1   2

3   4

4. This exercise is used in the Six Steps Workshop. Try it! Choose one of these shoes and answer the following questions, and come up with a great story! More about the workshop in figure 16 page 101.

a) Who owned this shoe?

b) Where did the owner get it?

c) Where did the owner walk in the shoe?

d) Where does the shoe end up?

EXERCISE

Read the first two pages of *Charlotte's Web*, close the book and rewrite the conversation between Fern and her father, coming as close as you can to E.B. White's words. Now compare the two versions of the same scene and you will see the strength in E.B. White's words and discover any weaknesses in your own.

president, much less get elected. However, if you have created an outgoing, unscrupulous boy, he might get himself elected by bending the rules. But perhaps his girlfriend, whom he hopes to impress, finds out about his secret deal and will have nothing more to do with him. And your shy guy? He's been in love with her all along and now when she looks around, there he is. Well, perhaps these are rather contrived characters and a thick plot, but they illustrate the important point that strong characters have a will of their own and can take over a plot.

When Louisa May Alcott wrote *Little Women*, her readers wanted Jo to marry Laurie, but Alcott knew that someone like her Jo could never marry a man like Laurie, and no matter how her readers begged, she refused to let it happen.

Dialogue is a powerful tool in characterization; it can also move your plot forward, show character development, and add to your story's credibility. Read some of the masters of dialogue in books(e.g., *Charlotte's Web* and *A Long Way from Chicago*) to see how they do it. Read your own dialogue to see if it is stilted or lacking character identification, and do the exercise at left.

PLOT

When you write your first draft, remember it is not set in cement. Just get it down on paper, and then you can fine-tune it, withholding information to create suspense, deleting parts that don't move your story along. You are very likely to get an idea when you are close to the end and you will have to change a large part of your story. If the change improves your story, make it.

A good editor will help you to say what you really mean but didn't know you knew. (See the advice of Andrea Cascardi, page 92 and Jennifer Weltz, page 113.) Careful polishing and self-editing will accomplish the same goal and possibly spell the difference between rejection and acceptance.

WRITING EXERCISE FOR TIME AND PLACE

Think back to a vivid experience you've had, and write a paragraph not about the experience, but describing the setting. If it is inside, describe the interior using specific details: fine furniture, lighting, etc. If it is outside, what was the weather like? The plants and trees? What are some telling details (e.g., the music being played) that might give the reader a sense of time and place?

PLOT EXERCISES

A Tulane student of children's literature, Jennifer Rosen, wrote this delightful, twisted "Cinderella."

Once upon a time I was a lonely widow with two daughters to raise. Life was hard for us, but luckily I was introduced to a wonderful widower with a daughter of his own. We had a storybook romance and were soon married. He and his daughter moved into our home. From the beginning, it was easy to see that Cinderella was going to be a handful. She was used to having her father all to herself and wanted a lot of attention. To be honest, she was a brat. She was a beautiful child, but she was vain and selfish and spent most of her day looking in the mirror. My own children were going through a gawky stage at the time. They wore glasses and braces and Cinderella showed off her good looks at them and made them feel ugly and horrible.

When Cinderella's father died, my problems really began. I took on two jobs to support the three girls. Everyone in the house had to pitch in with the chores. The day of that famous Ball it was Cindi's turn to scrub the floors. She refused and threw a fit instead and stormed out the door in a huff. My dear Griselda finished her own work and then finished Cinderella's.

As soon as Griselda put away the mop, there was a puff of smoke and the fairy godmother appeared. Cinderella wasn't even home! The fairy godmother had come to reward Griselda for being so kind to her mother. I remember her words. She said, "When you're beautiful inside, you are also beautiful outside." She waved her magic wand and suddenly Griselda's glasses and braces were gone. She was transformed into a beautiful princess complete with gown, diamond tiara and glass slippers. Off she went to the Ball in her horse-drawn pumpkin carriage.

It was Griselda, not Cinderella that captured the heart of the prince that night! They danced until the stroke of midnight. Griselda was so happy she forgot the fairy godmother's warning to return home by 12:00. Suddenly her pumpkin coach disappeared and she found herself standing in her old clothes. Naturally, she ran home as fast as she could, leaving her slipper behind on the stairs. She ran over four miles, so you can imagine how swollen her feet were when she finally got home! Cinderella got home about the same time as Griselda. She had spent the night feeling sorry for herself. When Griselda told her about the wonderful time she had at the Ball, Cinderella was furious that she had missed it. You could just see her anger behind her smile.

The next morning, the prince and his palace guards came to the door to see who fit the glass slipper that was left behind at the Ball. Griselda's feet were still so swollen she couldn't fit them into the shoe. In a flash, Cinderella snatched the slipper and slid it on her own foot. (Both girls wore exactly the same size.) I tried to explain the true story to the prince, but he didn't believe in fairy godmothers and magic wands. The rest of the tale is history. Cinderella and the prince were married. They didn't exactly live happily ever after. I understand the poor prince is miserable because Cinderella is still the same selfish girl she always was. I call all the time to try to see her, but she never returns my calls.

Please set the record straight. Tell everyone that stepmothers want more than anything to be loved by their new family. Sometimes it's stepchildren who stand in the way of that happiness. Often the problem is communication. Everyone is afraid to express true feelings. But only by working together could they truly live "happily ever after."

Put in its most simplistic form, a plot has a beginning, a middle, and an end. For the author, the beginning is usually the easiest, but difficulties may increase as you move toward a contrived ending. This progression is marked for the reader by increasing boredom and incredulity.

How many books have you read with great beginnings, bogged down middles, and incredible, manipulated endings? Here are some hints for avoiding these pitfalls:

- If you don't have a great beginning, read through your manuscript until you hit something interesting. Start there and lop off the preliminary part, bringing in any omitted, necessary information later on.

- Hook the reader on the first page or you'll lose him to TV, soccer, or worst of all, to another author's better book.

- Know where you're going, or rather, know where you can go if need be. Many's the promising beginning that was put aside because the author couldn't think of an ending. You don't have to stick to your preconceived ending, but it is comforting to have one.

- Make an outline or a plot summary, chapter by chapter. You don't have to stick to that either. In fact, your story will probably be better if you let your characters change things. But having your outline and knowing you have a strong story line will comfort you and see you through even if your final story has a different ending.

AVOIDING CLICHÉS (BERTHE)

I was fortunate when I started out to have one of the best children's book editors ever, Ursula Nordstrom of Harper & Row. The second picture book I did for her, *Tom in the Middle*, was about the plight of the middle child who has a bossy big brother and a pesky little one. Tom runs away from his brothers in my first version, pulling his "little red wagon." When Ursula read that, she said, "That's not what he'd really do, is it?" No, it's not," I said immediately. "He'd put on his beloved, outgrown policeman suit and he'd go to his secret place in the yard." *Tom in the Middle* is a much better book because the little red wagon cliché was dropped.

THE ANNOTATED TABLE OF CONTENTS (BERTHE AND ERIC)

When we started writing this book, our editors who had seen the first chapters and an outline made the suggestion that we should expand the case histories (then only one short paragraph each) and send them an "annotated table of contents," a much more detailed outline of what we intended to do in each chapter.

These suggestions were very helpful to us in organizing our vast amount of material into a cohesive whole. An important thing to remember is that an editor looking at your book professionally can see its strengths and weaknesses better than you can, and give you direction. Think twice before you reject the advice of an experienced editor or agent you'd like to represent you.

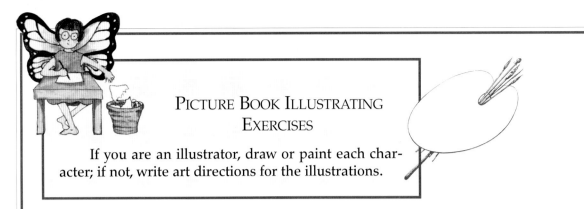

PICTURE BOOK ILLUSTRATING
EXERCISES

If you are an illustrator, draw or paint each character; if not, write art directions for the illustrations.

• The foggy, boggy middle: How to travel from a good idea to the perfect solution along an interesting path is not difficult if you've learned not to hang on to the first thought that crosses your mind. Play the "what if" game. Don't go down the obvious, trite, worn path in your mind. After you've done your first draft in a stream of consciousness style trying to get your ideas down, go over your writing looking for clichés in words, situations, and characters.

Get your ideas down in writing, and then let your story sit in your mind overnight, over many nights if necessary. The "right" path, fresh and untrodden, will appear to you, and when you take it, you'll have thought through the middle of your story and taken your reader with you.

The middle of your book is your place to develop your characters further and increase the depth of your plot, always aware of the tension that is needed between the beginning and the ending of your story. Don't forget: You can always delete great chunks of unwanted writing if parts don't further your story.

RESEARCH, RESEARCH, RESEARCH! (BERTHE)

After I'd written and illustrated several picture books, I fell in love with the written word and wanted to write a longer book. I wanted to write about the imaginary daughter of Marie Laveau, the Voo Doo queen, half-white and half-black, living in the wonderfully mixed culture of New Orleans in the 1840s. I was uncertain about writing a chapter book; I considered myself an illustrator, and even the short text of a picture book had not always come easily to me. But time and place fascinated me and I began reading firsthand accounts of life in New Orleans in the early and middle eighteenth century. I found collections of letters, reports, and two newspapers on microfilm at the Tulane library. Because my children were still small, I had little time. I did my writing in the wee hours of the morning and my research in the afternoon when they napped or played. The more I read, the more I wanted to read. I began to suspect that I'd missed a vocation — researcher. I felt very comfortable with my characters in the nineteenth century because now I knew what their world was like and what they thought about it.

EXERCISES

If you are writing a chapter book, make an annotated table of contents or plot summary for the book you are now writing. Divide the book into chapter headings, and under each heading, write a short summary of what happens in that chapter.

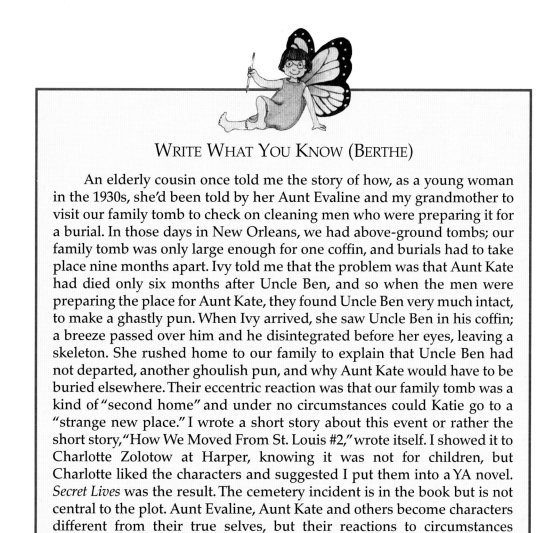

WRITE WHAT YOU KNOW (BERTHE)

An elderly cousin once told me the story of how, as a young woman in the 1930s, she'd been told by her Aunt Evaline and my grandmother to visit our family tomb to check on cleaning men who were preparing it for a burial. In those days in New Orleans, we had above-ground tombs; our family tomb was only large enough for one coffin, and burials had to take place nine months apart. Ivy told me that the problem was that Aunt Kate had died only six months after Uncle Ben, and so when the men were preparing the place for Aunt Kate, they found Uncle Ben very much intact, to make a ghastly pun. When Ivy arrived, she saw Uncle Ben in his coffin; a breeze passed over him and he disintegrated before her eyes, leaving a skeleton. She rushed home to our family to explain that Uncle Ben had not departed, another ghoulish pun, and why Aunt Kate would have to be buried elsewhere. Their eccentric reaction was that our family tomb was a kind of "second home" and under no circumstances could Katie go to a "strange new place." I wrote a short story about this event or rather the short story, "How We Moved From St. Louis #2," wrote itself. I showed it to Charlotte Zolotow at Harper, knowing it was not for children, but Charlotte liked the characters and suggested I put them into a YA novel. *Secret Lives* was the result. The cemetery incident is in the book but is not central to the plot. Aunt Evaline, Aunt Kate and others become characters different from their true selves, but their reactions to circumstances remained as they might have in real life.

SELF-EDITING CHECKLIST

PLACE: Does your writing give you a sense of place? What details in your writing could be true only in the place about which you are writing?

TIME: Does your writing "tell time?" What details could be true only in the time about which you are writing?

CHARACTERS: Ask the following questions about each of your characters:

1) Is this character "faceless," or does he/she seem like a real person?

2) Does the character always act "in character?"

3) Do your characters' actions determine your plot, or does your plot bend your characters out of shape?

PLOT: Does your story move forward relentlessly, or does it go off in different directions?

Does your story have suspense and tension, or is your ending predictable?

Is your story didactic? Remember that although you want your reader to come away from your book enriched, you do not want to write a little sermon to get your lesson across.

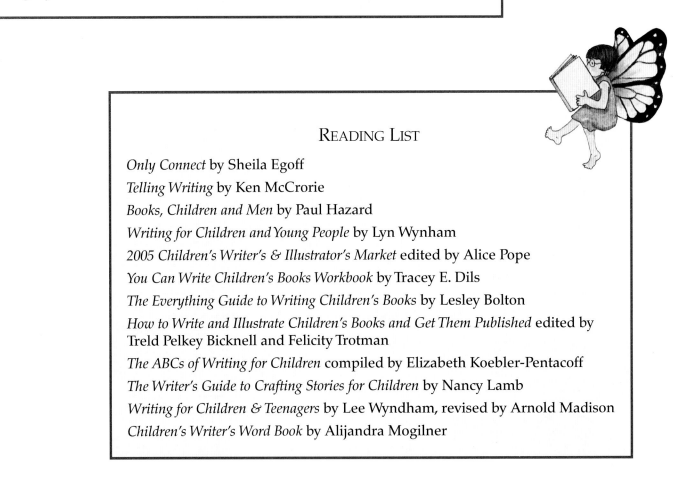

READING LIST

Only Connect by Sheila Egoff

Telling Writing by Ken McCrorie

Books, Children and Men by Paul Hazard

Writing for Children and Young People by Lyn Wynham

2005 Children's Writer's & Illustrator's Market edited by Alice Pope

You Can Write Children's Books Workbook by Tracey E. Dils

The Everything Guide to Writing Children's Books by Lesley Bolton

How to Write and Illustrate Children's Books and Get Them Published edited by Treld Pelkey Bicknell and Felicity Trotman

The ABCs of Writing for Children compiled by Elizabeth Koebler-Pentacoff

The Writer's Guide to Crafting Stories for Children by Nancy Lamb

Writing for Children & Teenagers by Lee Wyndham, revised by Arnold Madison

Children's Writer's Word Book by Alijandra Mogilner

Chapter 5

MAKING EVERY WORD COUNT

WRITING AND POLISHING

*I*t is said that writing cannot be taught, that writers are born, not made, but we believe that you can learn writing skills and that these will "free" you to write. Your own special creativity can be expressed only through and to the extent of your writing skills. In this chapter, we will show you how to acquire writing skills and how to polish your writing until every word counts.

LEARNING ABOUT WHAT'S GONE BEFORE

In many schools today, "creative writing" is taught in early, elementary grades before grammar. By third grade, children have made their own books. The theory is that writing helps reading. The downside of this approach is that children must eventually learn grammar rules or their power to communicate their ideas in writing is diminished. As we have said before, it is essential to produce a grammatically correct, neatly typed manuscript.

Rules must be learned so that you can break them, but you must learn them first. That is not as facetious as it sounds. Another way of putting it is: Grandchildren cannot come into the world before their parents and grandparents, and Maurice Sendak couldn't have written and illustrated *Where the Wild Things Are* before Wanda Gàg blazed the picture-book trail with *Millions of Cats*, the first true picture book in which the illustrations carry part of the story and are vital to an understanding and appreciation of the book as a whole.

It is important for you to know what has been done and what is being done in children's literature. If you have never had a survey course in children's literature, you should familiarize yourself now with what has been written for children in the past. At the end of this chapter, we have listed books to help guide your reading, and there are extensive lists of current and classic titles.

When you study children's literature, you will see that present-day books are built on the foundations of earlier books and that children's books reflect the times in which they were written. For example, you will notice that before World War II, many subjects were taboo in children's literature. Now there is scarcely a subject that has not been written about, from sex to drugs, although of course, controversial subject matter is handled with discretion. How you handle your subject matter will spell the difference between acceptance and rejection.

Notice, too, that in Victorian times, when children were meant to be seen and not heard, their books were filled with decorous role models, showing children formally dressed, and speaking and acting in proper, often stilted, style. Young villains, if they appeared at all, were presented without sympathy.

After World War II, along came Maurice Sendak, who, in *Where the Wild Things Are*, presented to the youngest reader the interior, dark side of his very own, young self. Other writers joined him in "telling it like it is" in children's books. Compare Maurice Sendak's twentieth-century illustrations of little people with Kate Greenaway's nineteenth-century ones for a stunning contrast.

THE ANATOMY OF A BOOK

If we could just figure out exactly what makes a book a best-seller and a classic, we'd be able to create one ourselves. It may not be possible to identify all the ingredients that will give us foolproof success: Indeed, some classics defy all the rules, such as E.B. White's *Charlotte's Web*, as mentioned earlier. However, if you examine a classic, any book that has stayed in print for 25 years, you will find clues that help you in your own writing.

One of the most important clues is that every classic has the children's stamp of approval on it; it has been chosen by children who, as Paul Hazard said in his *Books, Children and Men*, refuse to be bored by books. It doesn't matter how much hype the publisher, educator, or parent places on a book, a child will not read a book he doesn't like. But when children find one they love, they will claim it and hang on to it through generations — even if the book was not written for them, such as Daniel Defoe's *Robinson Crusoe*, and even when those adults who "know best" proclaim it unworthy of literature, such as all of Dr. Seuss and Judy Blume in the beginning. Study classics of the past to find the qualities with child appeal that you can apply to your own work.

We asked a 13-year-old boy what he looked for when choosing a book, hoping to identify clues to child appeal. Without hesitation, he said, "Suspense, mystery, and action!"

There are popular books that prove that a good book can come out of any genre and that classics often defy attempts at classification or anatomization.

There has to be something that keeps the reader turning the pages. Don't forget that young people will read only the books they want to read, and that the skill of writing good prose can be taught and learned.

CHARACTERS IN CHAPTER BOOKS AND YA NOVELS

Your characters must be well-rounded and believable in order to make the reader care about what happens to them. If you feel that your characters have blank faces or interchangeable faces, try writing a character study for each. Do this for your eyes alone. Try to visualize and write down everything you can think of about your character's appearance, disposition, family and peer situation. Get to know this person as you might a friend or family member. What are the problems your character faces? If you are writing a young adult novel, chances are it will encompass coming-of-age obstacles. What are they? What unique characteristics does your character have that will influence a response to these obstacles? Who are your character's peers and authority figures? Again going back to what we've said previously, your "real" characters will help you to plot your story. Real characters are the ones who will stay in the minds of readers and who can turn your book into a classic. Even if you are writing a picture book, your characters must still ring true.

SETTING

Once you have chosen your setting, be certain you know everything possible about it either through your own experience or meticulous research. Each setting has unique advantages and disadvantages. Make sure you understand them: One false move in a setting unfamiliar to you but lived in by your readers will destroy your credibility.

MYSTERY

If you are writing a mystery, the most important phases of your writing will be in the planning and polishing stages. In the planning stage, be sure you know how the mystery will be solved. Many is the promising mystery that has a disappointing ending because the writer did not figure out a believable, satisfying conclusion ahead of time. In the polishing stage, especially if yours is a story that almost wrote itself and that you were able to get down on paper quickly, read your story carefully, looking for places you can withhold information from your reader or mislead your reader (while at the same time maintaining the truth in the situation) into thinking in the wrong direction. You are aiming at an "Aha!" ending, one the reader must not suspect as he or she reads through the middle of the book.

SUSPENSE

Suspense is closely tied to mystery and tension. As your story progresses, the middle of your book is filled with obstacles, seemingly insurmountable, facing your protagonist. Again, be sure you, the writer, have figured out how those obstacles will be surmounted. Many times you will find that the solution is not readily visible to you. Don't give up. Let your plot problems simmer — for days, if necessary. The best, most exciting solutions are seldom the first you think of; they are usually the ones that occur to you suddenly, sometimes unexpectedly. That happens because your writing mind has been busy working on the problems while you were outwardly concerned with your daily life.

ACTION OR ADVENTURE

By now you will notice that mystery, suspense and action are so closely intertwined that they might all be included under the same umbrella and that ultimately that umbrella is characterization.

POLISHING

Go over your manuscript for mystery, suspense, and action, looking for information you give your reader too soon and for "red herrings" (false trails) you might add.

Make every word count. Go over your writing and remove all unnecessary adjectives, adverbs, and trite expressions. Get in the habit of rejecting the first descriptive word that comes into your head. If you don't have to say it, don't; if you do, make your reader hear or see it.

We are, of course, assuming that you will check your manuscript for grammar, spelling, and typos. If you are shaky in these areas, use your computer's capabilities or ask a literate friend to copy-edit for you. Never let a manuscript leave your hands unless it is the best you can do.

THE ANATOMY OF A PICTURE BOOK

There is no better way to learn than to scrutinize the work of published authors. Trying persistently to figure out how that other writer did it can be helpful, though it can sometimes diminish the joy of reading if you practice it constantly.

Here are a few from the many classics you can "dissect," looking for what makes them beloved:

Goodnight Moon (perhaps the most difficult to analyze)
Where the Wild Things Are
Chicka Chicka Boom Boom
Brown Bear, Brown Bear, What Do You See?
Millions of Cats
The Tale of Peter Rabbit
If You Give a Mouse a Cookie
The Cat in the Hat
Olivia

In studying the anatomy of books, or what gives them child appeal, you will notice that the reader is drawn in by identifying with a character or perceiving a familiar situation. There may be an obstacle one of the characters successfully surmounts. To paraphrase Bruno Bettelheim in his *The Uses of Enchantment,* there is, hidden in the tale, something that helps a child find meaning in life. Too lofty? Doesn't encompass books meant to amuse only? Yes, it does. Stretching the imagination, exposure to visual art, humor, are all necessary to cognitive growth.

In classics, you will notice that there is also a strong theme and a tension that keeps the reader turning pages. Try to identify the theme.

In traditional art schools, students learn the basics of drawing and painting by studying the Old Masters. They draw from life and from plaster busts, learning about composition, value, shape, and design, and they sit in museums and paint copies of masterpieces, trying to discover how the artist did it. This method of learning, applied to studying the classics, can help writers as they try to communicate their own ideas to readers through writing and illustrating.

Think of this applied learning technique as a course entitled The Anatomy of a Book. For example, let us consider *Millions of Cats*, by Wanda Gàg. Wanda Gàg knew and loved the classic fairy tales of the Brothers Grimm. She helped raise her

EXERCISES

- Choose a classic picture book (a book in print for more than 25 years). Do an anatomy of it.

- Where does an illustration carry part of the story line not in the text?

- Summarize the plot.

- Look for clues that you believe have made this book a classic. In short, how did one illustrator/artist do it? Do an anatomy of your own book in dummy form, and correct what you perceive to be faults.

- If you are writing a longer chapter book or a young adult novel for children, you can apply the same anatomy-of-a-book technique using your favorite book in that genre.

Notice how the text is "hand-written." How would the page look if Gàg had used a type-face? Find a double spread (an illustration that stretches across two pages). How does this help the flow of the story? It is said that when her books were being printed, Gàg supervised and insisted that the black must be black and not a faded, dark dark gray! How does she keep her illustrations from crying out for color? Compare an old fairy tale in its original form (not adapted or changed, but translated) and notice the following characteristics shared by *Millions of Cats*: No particular time, no specific place, no characterization, all information needed in first paragraph. Look at the illustrations in an early nineteenth-century book and notice the similarities: no color, simple, usually narrative as well as decorative. To appreciate fully the artistry of *Millions of Cats*, try imagining this book in full color with typeset and an embellished text (adjectives, adverbs and descriptions). For more insight into illustration and love of language, look for *Tales from Grimm*, lovingly translated from the German and illustrated by Wanda Gàg.

orphaned sisters and brothers, and so she knew, too, what children liked. Her parents had been artists, and she became a printmaker in the twenties when that art form had a renaissance in this country and when publishers first opened departments solely devoted to children's books.

Millions of Cats is probably the first true American picture book in which the illustrations play as large a role as the text.

Here is an anatomical study of the writing of *Millions of Cats* (the illustrations are discussed in Chapter 6):

1) The story begins like a folk or fairy tale with "once upon a time" and all the information the reader needs summarized on the first page.

2) There is no characterization. We know only that an old man and an old woman are childless and lonely.

3) Still on the first page, and in the first paragraph, we learn the entire situation: The old man will go on a journey to find a cat to cure their loneliness.

4) Again like the folk tale, the setting is any place and our time is any time. There is very little setting description.

5) The simplicity of the story line and the clean prose throughout - not an extra word anywhere — gives this picture book its classic quality.

WRITING THE TEXT OF A PICTURE BOOK

If you are writing a picture book, it may help you to think of this genre as similar to poetry and your book as an illustrated prose poem. Obviously, your text must be short like a poem to accommodate a very young child's short attention span. Each word of a poem or picture book is important to express as clearly and as richly as possible your idea. That limitation forces you to choose words carefully and to eliminate ruthlessly words that are unnecessary. Again, like a poem, there should be only one simple idea, and every word must contribute to expressing that idea to make it comprehensible at a young child's level of experience. A four year old, for example, might not understand the evils of war, but he can be shown that it is cruel to kick a dog.

WRITING THE TEXT OF A CHAPTER BOOK

Because the text of a picture book, typed and double-spaced, is usually not much more than two pages long, it is obvious that every word counts; but if you are writing a book for older children, it is also true, although not as obvious. Read the first two pages of E.B. White's *Charlotte's Web*, then close the book, and in your own words, write that much of the story. When you reread White's version, you will be more aware of his clean, concise prose, the power and depth of his communication. Fern sees the situation from a child's point of view: It isn't fair to kill a pig just because he's the runt of a litter. Then you see the situation from her parents' point of view: Fern has to grow up, they are thinking, and learn that sometimes things in life are necessary even though they are not fair.

DIALOGUE AND LANGUAGE

Notice the dialogue on those two pages. The characters talk like real people, and the story is carried along and characterization developed within the quotation marks.

Nancy Willard's *The Sorceror's Apprentice* is another excellent book to study for an appreciation of the richness of language. Extravagantly designed and gorgeously illustrated by Leo and Diane Dillon, what child (or adult) would not fall in love at first sight with Sylire, the apprentice, and tremble with delectable fear at Willard's word picture:

"The house had fifty-seven doors
That snapped and growled
And groaned and roared,
And Knockers made of gnashing teeth,
Which mercifully hung out of reach."

But where are the adjectives? How does Willard give us such a vivid image? How does she tell the entire story always choosing the right word and never forcing a rhyme? Pore over this book, enjoying and thinking about how it's done.

There are many old and modern classics to read and learn from, and the more you study, the more you'll understand what makes a classic and how you can turn your own ideas into good books for children.

Beth Woods
Education 614
Professor Amoss
October 6, 1993

Children's Rhymes

I won't go to Macy's no more no more.

There's a big fat policeman by the door door door.

He grabbed me by the collar, and he made me pay a dollar,

So I won't go to Macy's no more no more.

WRITING EXERCISE

Select a nursery rhyme you remember hearing when you were a child, or one you've heard recently from a child. It shouldn't be one you've seen in a book but rather has been passed from child to child, such as a skip-rope rhyme. Give it a twist of your own (make it more contemporary or change it in some way) and do an original line drawing to go with it (yes, draw even if you're not an illustrator!). Pictured left is an example by a Tulane student of children's literature.

MORE POLISHING

After you've written your story, perhaps in a stream-of-consciousness style, you may find it is just the way you want it to be. Double-check it for tense discrepancies, trite adjectives that are so overused they have lost their power (beautiful, awesome, great, happy), and stock phrases (quick as a wink, skinny as a rail). Look for wordy, boring explanations of things that can be shown in an illustration, left unsaid, or shown through dialogue, such as, "She had a winning smile" or "She sighed in resignation."

Every time you come across an adverb or an adjective, think about it. Does it convey anything? Could it be translated into a verb: "She ran fast" into "She raced"?

Complex sentences that confuse rather than clarify, run-on sentences, paragraphs that never end may seem unimportant in your grand plan of the whole book, but a reading editor does not have time to teach you basic writing skills and will usually reject a sloppily written manuscript, even if it has the possibilities of becoming a good book.

Take advantage of your readers' senses of taste, smell, sight, and feel. Don't tell your reader the landscape is beautiful; describe it so that the reader believes she is in that place. Don't tell your reader the hero of your book felt sad; instead, describe what has caused the hero's feelings.

In the theater, there is a tradition that a tragic actor must never cry; the actor must make the audience weep (e.g., Charlotte's death in *Charlotte's Web*).

SELF-EDITING CHECKLIST

Check your manuscript for:

1) spelling and grammatical errors

2) unnecessary or meaningless words

3) tension

4) satisfying ending

5) Are you writing about something you care deeply about that comes from a child-like point of view?

6) Has it the power to expand a child's vision and understanding of the world?

7) Does it involve the young reader's participation, either verbal, mental, or physical?

8) Will it enhance the child's cognitive or creative abilities?

9) Will it appeal to a child, attract and hold his attention, or have you allowed yourself to be carried away by something you want a child to know?

READING LIST

Many of these books are out-of-print, but they can be found in your library. We continue to list them because they are so good and helpful.

Telling Writing by Ken Macrorie
The Uses of Enchantment by Bruno Bettelheim
Only Connect by Sheila Egoff
Children's Books in England by Harvey Darton
The Classic Fairy Tales by Iona and Peter Opie
Writing With Pictures by Uri Shulevitz
The Annotated Mother Goose by William Baring-Gould
Three Centuries of Books in Europe by Bettina Hurlimann
Children and Literature by John Warren Steurg
The Arbuthnot Anthology of Children's Literature by May Hill Arbuthnot
Books, Children and Men by Paul Hazard
Writing for Children and Teenagers by Lee Wyndham

CLASSICS OF THE SEVENTEENTH THROUGH NINETEENTH CENTURIES

Perrault's Fairy Tales 1697
Robinson Crusoe by Daniel Defoe 1719
Gulliver's Travels by Jonathan Swift 1726
A Little Pretty Pocket-Book by John Newbery 1744
A Visit from St. Nicholas by Clement Moore 1822
Grimm's Popular Stories in English (trans. Edgar Taylor) 1823
A Christmas Carol by Charles Dickens 1843
Fairy Tales by Hans Christian Andersen 1846
Alice's Adventures in Wonderland by Lewis Carroll 1865
Little Women by Louisa M. Alcott 1868
The Adventures of Tom Sawyer by Mark Twain 1876
Treasure Island by Robert Louis Stevenson 1883
Robin Hood by Howard Pyle 1883
Heidi by Johanna Spyri 1884
The Adventures of Huckleberry Finn by Mark Twain 1884
The Jungle Book by Rudyard Kipling 1894

TREND-SETTING BOOKS OF THE TWENTIETH CENTURY

The Tale of Peter Rabbit by Beatrix Potter 1901
Millions of Cats by Wanda Gàg 1928
Where the Wild Things Are by Maurice Sendak 1963

Chapter 6

ILLUSTRATION

The turn of the century — which produced such great illustrators as Howard Pyle, N.C. Wyeth, and Arthur Rackham — is often called "The Golden Age of Illustration," but if any period of time challenges the title, it is ours. Children's books today are of unsurpassed quality and diversity.

Books are an art form. With or without illustrations, books can be pleasing to the eye, and the content can move the reader in some profound way. Especially with children, a book can exert a powerful, developmental influence. In *The Uses of Enchantment*, Bruno Bettelheim wrote that potentially, books rank third after parents and educators in helping children find meaning in life.

Authors, illustrators, and editors almost always think of their books as works of art. Great care is taken with the format, the quality of the paper, the typeface, the binding, cover and jacket, and the illustrations if any. Of course, the aesthetics have to be balanced with cost and marketing factors, but there is something about a book that has always attracted people who care about art. Most fine artists at one time or another try their hand at a one-of-a-kind book, as art for art's sake, and book lovers (your authors included) are among the most avid of collectors.

If you are creating a book, seeing it as an art form and understanding the possibilities of what can go into it are important steps toward a successful presentation to a publisher.

In this chapter, we will examine three very different books as art forms: *Millions of Cats* by Wanda Gàg, *The Animal Family* by Randall Jarrell and "decorated" by Maurice Sendak, and *Pish, Posh, Said Hieronymous Bosch* by Nancy Willard, illustrated by Leo and Diane Dillon.

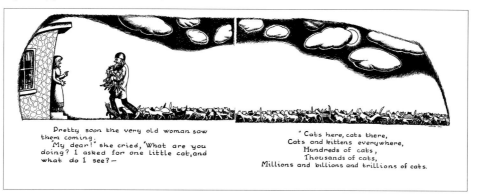

Pretty soon the very old woman saw them coming.
"My dear!" she cried, "What are you doing? I asked for one little cat, and what do I see? —

" Cats here, cats there,
Cats and kittens everywhere,
Hundreds of cats,
Thousands of cats,
Millions and billions and trillions of cats.

Millions of Cats, written and illustrated by Wanda Gàg in 1928, is considered the first true American picture book, if you accept our definition that the illustrations play as important a role as the text in the book as a whole.

We can learn almost all we have to know about picture books from this simple little story with its black-and-white illustrations. We recommend you either buy an inexpensive copy or check one out from your library.

Wanda Gàg was born in the closely knit, culturally German community of Ulm, Minnesota, around the turn of the twentieth century. Her father, a painter, and her sickly mother both died when Gàg, the oldest of five children, was still a teenager. She refused the kind offers of several families to take the children into their homes, and kept her siblings together, supporting them by doing odd jobs such as painting lampshades. She saw to it that they all received an education, which included familiarity with her beloved Grimm's fairy tales. Later, Gàg lived with a family as the nanny to their children and entertained them with her own stories and drawings. She became a recognized artist, a printmaker at a time when printmaking was having a renaissance and publishers were just beginning to see a need for more children's books. When an editor saw Wanda's work in a gallery show and asked her to produce a picture book, she had already written and illustrated *Millions of Cats* for the family of children she had lived with. It was published and was an instant success.

Millions of Cats is a picture book of 32 pages, with the illustrations carrying part of the plot and integral to the text. The text, in Gàg's cursive writing, is really a part of her page composition along with her black-and-white, woodcut-like drawings, neatly composed on the page. The illustrations flow between the pages, carrying the eye from page to page. Each page is carefully composed as a whole composition or two pages form a double spread (at that time, a new concept in books for children), one that takes the eye over the "gutter" (the separation made by the seam where the two pages meet) and joins the two pages in a complete picture.

In the illustrations we see the little cat grow fatter and cuter until it becomes pretty and cuddly. And that is it: a very simple idea, cozy little black-and-white drawings, and pages that make a whole art object.

THE HUNTER

The Animal Family by Randall Jarrell was not illustrated but rather "decorated" by Maurice Sendak. This is a remarkable collaboration of artists, both of whom loved the old fairy tales — not just the stories but the language and German culture of the early nineteenth century. They agreed that the text should not be illustrated; the reader could better imagine the images from the text. Sendak's ink drawings are all of inanimate objects. The theme of the book is the warmth of family and everything about the book contributes to establishing a feeling of contentment and security. The poetic text is like a happy dream, part fantasy, part ideal realism, and is surrounded by wide borders that seem to hold the words as the walls of a small, cozy house might hold a family. The story itself is not sentimental but it is comforting, unassuming, and full of wisdom, the beautiful vision of a poet, which Jarrell was. The paper is a fine quality and the type elegant yet simple. The size of the book is small and the shape a square. It is the kind of book you give to someone you love, and it is the kind of book that demonstrates a book without real illustrations can still be a work of art. This book is still in print and can be ordered from your local bookstore.

Pish, Posh, Said Hieronymous Bosch (pictured on page 112) by Nancy Willard with illustrations by Leo and Diane Dillon (and a frame sculpted by their artist son) is the ultimate children's-book-as-an-art-form. It brings together an acclaimed poet/writer (her book *A Visit to William Blake's Inn* won the Newbery Medal) and two award-winning illustrators (the Dillons were twice awarded the Caldecott Medal for their incomparably lovely illustrations).

Hieronymous Bosch was a Flemish, fifteenth-century artist, wildly imaginative and known particularly for his bizarre, surreal visions of heaven and hell. Willard's story-poem is witty, delightful and matches Bosch in imaginative creation. The Dillons designed as well as illustrated the book; you can imagine the publishers saying, "It's all yours! Do what you want and make it a great work of art!" The text is hand-lettered, and shot as a halftone so as to preserve the shadings of tone in the calligraphic letters. The paper is especially fine and heavy, and the entire book very beautiful by any standards.

These three books, each so different from the others, are all nevertheless worth studying as art forms. If you are not an illustrator, you will probably have little say about how your text is illustrated, but keeping in mind how closely related text, design, and illustration are in books for young people, an understanding of the whole book and a good background in visual literacy will enhance your chances of producing a publishable manuscript.

Here are some other books we think are worth careful study on your part:

- *Zlateh the Goat* by Isaac Bashevis Singer and illustrated by Maurice Sendak is a book of short stories for children, an illustrated book, not a picture book. Although Singer said illustrations might inhibit the reader from forming his own pictures in the imagination, that may be an Old World view, not applicable to today's children. These ink drawings are Sendak at his best, and he captures the spirit of the East European Jewish culture that disappeared in the Holocaust. Examine this book for its unforgettable stories, powerful use of language, and the best of the best illustrations that interpret but do not carry the plot. Notice the difference between these illustrations and Sendak's *Where the Wild Things Are*, where the illustrations do carry the plot.

- All of the books illustrated by the Dillons, particularly *The Sorcerer's Apprentice* by Nancy Willard.

- All of the books written by Nancy Willard. Different illustrators have illustrated her books of poetry and prose, all are well-known and have different styles. Decide for yourself which combinations make the best whole books!

- *Alice in Wonderland* and *Through the Looking Glass* by Lewis Carroll. No matter how many wonderful artists illustrate this classic, and there have been many, including Walt Disney, Tenniel's original illustrations are so much a part of the text that they remain the way we see Alice and her world.

- *Winnie-the-Pooh* by A.A. Milne with illustrations by E.H. Shepherd is another book with illustrations married to the text in spite of Disney's popular interpretations. A learning experience is to compare E.H. Shepherd's illustrations with Disney's animated characters and see how close they are and what the differences are. Then try to figure out why the changes were made.

Finding Time (Berthe)

One of my most precious possessions is a copy of the illustrated letter Lena de Grummond received from Edward Ardizzone, my hero of illustration. He explained to her that he could not break up a set of his illustrations to send her one, but if ever she was in London, he invited her to stop by for a cup of tea. He didn't know Lena. She took him up on his invitation and returned to USM with a whole set of Ardizzone illustrations. The Lena de Grummond collection of children's literature is one of the top collections in the country.

CASE HISTORY: LISBETH ZWERGER

On a crisp September morning in 1983, I took the subway to a suburb of Vienna to see Lisbeth Zwerger. It had taken all of my courage and rusty German to call from the hotel and

ask for an interview. I expected to see a middle-aged, worldly woman used to fame and fortune. After all, Zwerger had received a gold medal at the Biennial International of Illustration in Bratislava, two graphic prizes at the Bologna Children's Book Fair, and a *New York Times* citation for one of their "Ten Best Illustrated Books of 1982." When I got out of the subway in a nonplush neighborhood of shops and large apartment buildings, I wondered if I'd gotten the wrong address. But there was no. 7 and "Zwerger" was written under one of the 20 doorbells. I climbed the steps and on the fifth floor, the door opened. Surely, this was Liz Zwerger's teenage daughter who showed me into a bright, contemporary living room with a large sofa, a wall of books, and an uncluttered artist's desk near the window.

But the young lady who looked like Audrey Hepburn in *Roman Holiday* was Liz Zwerger herself and it didn't take me long to realize that she was timid and as nervous as I was. I began by asking her how she became an illustrator. She told me she had been such a poor student that the only thing she could do was go to art school. But that answer like everything else about her was far too modest, and it came out later in our conversation that she had shown unusual talent as a child and that her father was a graphic artist. She had always loved Grimm, Andersen, and Hoffmann, and her favorite illustrator

was Arthur Rackham. At art school, her teacher urged her to go into fine art, but she was only interested in illustration. I asked her if she wouldn't like to write her own stories as many illustrators in the United States do, but she said she preferred thinking about stories already written and channeling all of her creativity into art. Zwerger's paintings are the same size as the reproduced illustrations, and she does them in watercolor on watercolor paper. Her composition is striking. She uses lots of space around her figures and unusual perspective. Her colors are earthy; even her blue has warmth. The backgrounds are wash, and the figures more opaque and drawn in a brown ink line. She uses the kind of drawing pen you dip into ink, the kind of nib that separates slightly when pressure is applied and produces a line of varying thickness, the kind you see in Hogarth and Daumier's work. It requires confidence and absolute control, no timid strokes. I asked her if she used models because her figures show such a thorough knowledge of anatomy but she said only when she has to draw furniture or animals. Lisbeth Zwerger is an illustrator who keeps alive the tradition of creating books as an art form and gives you insight into the "anatomy of success."

You may prefer one artist to another, but never make the mistake of thinking one style is necessarily better than another. The beauty of contemporary illustration is in its diversity and the wonderful technology that allows printers to reproduce full color so accurately and provide children with a variety of good art. If you want to become visually literate, base your critical perception of the art on the plastic values: line, color, texture, pattern, form, and composition. It is not enough to simply like an illustration or not like it. In order to be the best creator of children's books you can be, you should know why you like or dislike an illustration.

Notice the format, the quality of the paper, the binding, everything that is part of the book. It may be that the art is poorly reproduced or that the quality of the paper is so bad, it dulls the colors. Great illustration can be rendered boring and blurry by poor reproduction.

The following list of books can serve you as a mini-survey of the history of children's-book illustration. You will encounter a wide selection of illustrative styles, get an idea of the times, and find clues as to what makes a children's classic.

EIGHTEENTH CENTURY: CHAPBOOKS, HORNBOOKS, AND BATTLEDORES:

The earliest books exclusively for children were really textbooks to teach them numbers, the alphabet, and moral lessons. Chapbooks — inexpensive, crudely printed books — were for adults but many of them were appropriated by children starved for story. They were illustrated, if at all, by woodcuts. You will see fine examples of early illustration in Peter and Iona Opie's *The Oxford Dictionary of Nursery Rhymes*. *The Classic Fairy Tales* by the same authors includes excellent examples of eighteenth-and nineteenth-century illustration. If you intend to add to your library, these two books are great choices for understanding the roots of children's literature.

NINETEENTH-CENTURY ILLUSTRATORS:

George Cruiskhank, *Grimm's Popular Stories and Oliver Twist*
Edward Lear, *Book of Nonsense*
Kate Greenaway, *Under the Window*
Walter Crane, *Sing a Song of Sixpence*
Randolph Caldecott, *The House That Jack Built*
John Tenniel, *Alice's Adventures in Wonderland*
Howard Pyle, *The Merry Adventures of Robin Hood*

TWENTIETH-CENTURY ILLUSTRATORS, FIRST HALF:

Leslie Brooke, *Johnny Crow's Garden*
Beatrix Potter, *The Tale of Peter Rabbit*
N.C. Wyeth, *The Scottish Chiefs*
Jessie Willcox Smith, *A Child's Garden of Verses*
Kay Nielsen, *East of the Sun and West of the Moon*
Maxfield Parrish, *Arabian Nights*
Edmund Dulac, *Fairy Book*
Arthur Rackham, *Hawthorne's Wonder Book*
Kate Seredy, *The Good Master*
E.H. Shepherd, *The Wind in the Willows*
Wanda Gàg, *Millions of Cats*
Maud and Miska Petersham, *Heidi*

After World War II, modern printing techniques and the children's-book field exploded with a wealth of diverse, marvelous illustrators too numerous to list. If you are interested in studying more about the history of children's illustration, there are many reference books in your library.

When you come to contemporary styles, don't confuse classic with trend. What's popular today is likely to be passé or dated tomorrow; it's what the best-sellers have in common that you can incorporate into your own work. We see bright, clear colors, concise text, and simplicity in books for the youngest; a bit older, children are reading by themselves and delight in the world around them. They are little sponges for knowledge and in illustration they see detail and don't like confusion. Still older children want action, mystery, adventure, and characters they can empathize with, role models, situations in the plot that mirror their own and help them to see solutions. They still like illustration in their books provided the illustrations don't make the books look juvenile. Still older children have more definite taste: they like realism, fantasy, science fiction, even historical fiction as long as it doesn't play down to them or bore them.

Caution: Avoid imitation! Your study of books as an art form is meant to bring out the best in you. You are looking for inspiration and the best way to express your own ideas most effectively. Don't imitate a style in hopes of pleasing a child or an editor; look for new approaches that bring out what is uniquely yours.

Studying books as an art form translates into understanding how you can make your own book irresistible to a publisher.

Patsy H. Perritt, Professor Emeritus, School of Library and Information Science, Louisiana State University, has contributed the following sections on Visual Literacy, Picture Book Format, and Mediums.

VISUAL LITERACY THROUGH PICTURE BOOKS

Just hearing words and finally learning to read adds immeasurably to a child's world.

Children can be guided in the process of learning to read; they can also be guided in the appreciation of visual images. What better way to develop "visual literacy" than in the books they might already love or the books they might easily obtain in their schools and libraries?

This section will cover book design and mediums for preparing art, as well as some descriptions of the picture-book format that might be helpful in the preparation of illustration as well as useful to those seeking to guide children in "visual literacy."

As an author, it is important to know that you are not responsible for providing an illustrated manuscript. The publisher will employ an illustrator, and as strange as it might seem, most often the author and the illustrator do not collaborate. The publisher also employs an art director, who usually works with the illustrator from earliest stages of creation to the final printing. The art director guides such decisions as size of the book; weight, color, and texture of the paper; typography; cover art and flap copy; placement of words and text; frontispiece and tailpiece material and illustration, as well as endpapers.

If you are an artist and you want to illustrate books for children, here are some basics of children's picture-book illustration and book design that will help you to get started in the field.

THE PICTURE-BOOK FORMAT

LENGTH:

The standard length of a picture book is 32 pages in total. That means the illustrator has the back and front of 16 pages to use, and those pages will include the half-title page, title pages (usually a double page), and another page for publisher's information and CIP (Cataloging-in-Publication) data. It is possible to utilize the endpapers, which are the back of the hard cover, referred to as "boards," and the page next to it in the front of the book and in the back of the book, but only for visual "suggestion," not for text. Decorative end papers are expensive and are not used on all books, but even the color and texture of end papers can enhance the mood of the story.

SIZE:

Consider the average size of a bookshelf, approximately ten inches deep and 12 inches high. Most publishers encourage a book size that will easily fit on a library shelf with the spine facing out and discourage wide diversion, such as long, skinny shapes that would stick out from a shelf, very small sizes that would easily get lost behind other books; or tall books that would have to be placed on a shelf by turning the book on its side. You will need to consider the feeling that you wish to create within the viewer. Do the words need visuals that reinforce a sense of vastness, or coziness, or towering heights? Take a careful look at a variety of sizes and shapes, and ask yourself "Why is this size or shape important/appropriate to the telling of the story?" (See Wanda Gàg's *Millions of Cats*, Don and Audrey Woods's *The Napping House*, and any of the Beatrix Potter tales in their original, small-book size.) The illustrations need to be in close proximity to the words being illustrated. There is no "right" way to place the illustrations, such as above or below the words. The illustrator must decide what is suitable placement for the mood and flow of the visual presentation. A child who is learning to "read" visuals in a book needs a straight-forward, one-scene presentation, such as Nancy Tafuri's *Have You Seen My Ducklings?* or Lois Ehlert's *Feathers for Lunch*. In planning the page layout, always remember the technical reality of the "gutter," the portion of the paper taken up by the binding. Allow at least one-quarter inch on the inner edge of each page for stitching, and design any double-page spread to accommodate the visual impact of the gutter. Never have the focal point of a two-page spread in the exact center of the double page or it will be "swallowed" in the gutter

when the pages are bound. The illustration should be so composed that the viewer's eye will not be stopped by the strong vertical line created by the gutter.

STYLE AND SIZE OF TYPE:

An art director or book designer will provide guidance in the selection of typeface, size, and color, but you can offer suggestions as to why a particular style, size, and color seem to be in harmony with the story being told. Numerous samples can be found by inquiring at a local printing company, consulting books on typography and graphic design, or even by experimenting with the various fonts and sizes on personal computers. Legibility is always the key factor, but there is a range of possibilities in style, size, and color of the print.

BOOK JACKET AND COVER:

Some picture books have separate paper covers or illustrated hard covers that could require additional illustrations. The first illustration seen by a potential reader must have persuasive powers. It must raise questions as to what might be happening within the book, thereby drawing the reader to open the book. The illustrator should consider the interest that could be initiated on the cover, proceeding across the endpapers to the half-title page and on to the title pages, possibly including the page for publishing and cataloging information.

DIFFERENT JACKETS (BERTHE)

When I saw the jacket for my young adult novel, *Secret Lives*, I fell in love with it. The original artwork was an elegant, large watercolor showing the interior of a Victorian living room with the three main characters in it. It seemed to me that the artist had interpreted everything I had tried to say in the text. It was a beautiful painting and looked mysterious, old-fashioned and intriguing. Two years later the paperback edition came out with a different cover showing an Afro-American girl and a white one rummaging through an old trunk in the attic. Again, another artist had caught the spirit of the book but this cover had a Nancy Drew look to it, promising mystery and excitement and was exactly right for the paperback market. Both very different jackets of the same book were great hooks, and the paperback went into three editions before it went out of print.

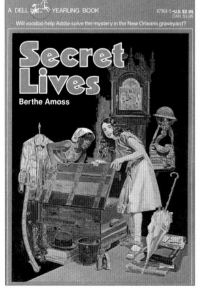

MEDIUMS:

Today's reproduction technology allows the use of almost any medium and technique in illustration. Everything from quilts to relief sculptures can be photographed, the colors separated by laser scanner, and then painted. The following examples show the infinite range of media being used, often in combination within a single illustration, to create a spectrum of visual effects:

WATERCOLORS – *The Little Mermaid*, illustrated by Jerry Pinkney

OILS – *Rapunzel*, illustrated by Paul O. Zelinksy

ACRYLICS – *Westlandia*, illustrated by Kevin C. Hawkes

INK – *Millions of Cats*, illustrated by Wanda Gàg

PENCIL – *Jumanji*, illustrated by Chris Van Allsburg

PLASTICINE – *Two by Two* and *Have You Seen Birds?*, illustrated by
     Barbara Reid Wood

METAL – *Aida*, illustrated by Leo and Diane Dillon
     (metal frame created by Lee Dillon)

TISSUE PAPER – *Eric Carle's Animals Animals*, illustrated by Eric Carle

CUT PAPER – *Rain Player*, illustrated by David Wisniewski; *The Paper Crane*,
     illustrated by Molly Bang

PAPER PULP – *In the Small Small Pond* and *In the Tall Tall Grass*,
     illustrated by Denise Fleming

FABRIC – *Tar Beach*, illustrated by Faith Ringgold (see borders)

The techniques, or methods of creating the art, are equally varied and often combined, including painting, etching, wood and linoleum cutting, airbrush, collage, photography, and computer imagery:

AIRBRUSH – *Why Mosquitoes Buzz in People's Ears*, illustrated by Leo and Diane
     Dillon

COLLAGE – *Pie in the Sky* by Lois Ehlert

PHOTOGRAPHY – *Spots, Feathers, and Curly Tails*, illustrated by Tana Hoban

The following section is written and illustrated by Auseklis Ozols, founder and head of the prestigious New Orleans Academy of Fine Arts. It is based on his course, Color and Design, in which he teaches students principles of art as applicable to illustration as they are to fine art.

A MINI-COURSE IN COLOR AND DESIGN

THE PLASTIC VALUES

The *plastic values* are the aesthetic tools of the artist. They are line, color, value, texture, pattern, and form.

1) LINE: In reality, line does not actually exist, but the artist uses a pencil or pen line to indicate the beginning and end of particular shapes.

The overlapping of two different values creates an implied line (figures 1 and 2). Drawn line expresses the temperament and character of individual artists. Line quality is a condition that is imparted to the drawn line that renders it unique in expression.

As an exercise, draw a fast line, a slow one, angry, nervous, brittle, soft, lyrical, bombastic.

Figure 1: The density of the dots create the sense of space as well as mass and line.

Complete compositions can be executed in only line, as in pencil and pen-and-ink drawings, etchings, engravings etc.

Linear perspective (figure 3) is the two-dimensional representation of the third dimension. It is the study of the natural phenomenon where objects decrease in size as they recede farther back in space. The laws governing perspective require greater space than allowed here (suggested reading: Perspective for Artists by Rex Vicat Cole, Dover [22487-2].)

2) COLOR: The visible spectrum is like the rainbow: It starts with red, orange, yellow, green, blue, and violet, and it includes all transition colors. The color wheel was devised by bending the spectrum around until the red and violet connect.

Color may be the most expressive element of the plastic values. The moods and emotions that can be expressed by color are

Figure 2: The outline of this sphere and its shadow are not delineated by a line, and the values therein are not created by tone but by intersecting line.

Figure 3: Linear perspective is the study of the natural phenomenon where objects decrease in size as they recede farther back in space.

legion (see The Terminology of Color, on page 63 and the color wheel (figure 6, page 97).

3) VALUE: An important corollary of color, value refers to the relation of a color to black-and-white and all the grays in between. By mixing white or black with a color, we change its value without changing its hue, which we indicate by saying light blue or dark blue. The knowledge of a scale of grays from white to black is indispensable to the artist (figure 4).

COLOR PERSPECTIVE – Air, as well as water, is a substance composed of molecules, and it takes on specific color dependent upon the light quality of the day or time of day. On a cloudless, sunny day, the air color is blue, which reflects on everything it contains. On overcast days, the air color can be a variety of grays, during a sunset it can be orange, and so on. Color perspective is the expression of distance and space by the addition of air color to pictorial elements. The more air color is added, the further in distance objects appear. The combination of linear and color perspective enhance greatly the sense of space.

4) TEXTURE: Texture is a visual as well as tactile sensation. It is surface quality attributed to certain objects. Sand has its texture, the bark of a tree another, etc. We can express differences in texture by use of variance in line quality and different techniques of pigment application.

5) PATTERN: Pattern is a repetition of a shape or combination of shapes. Any single shape, no matter how insignificant in appearance, when repeated in a regular manner, will create a lovely pattern. Pattern greatly enriches the visual dynamics of design.

6) FORM Form is a loose term applied to the perception of mass or volume, or the idea of solid objects in the third dimension.

Figure 4: Value refers to the relation of a color to black and white and all the grays in between. In order to change the value of a color, we must mix it with something lighter or darker than itself.

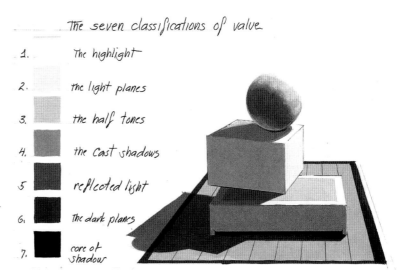

The seven classifications of value

1. The highlight
2. the light planes
3. the half tones
4. the cast shadows
5. reflected light
6. The dark planes
7. core of shadow

61

COMPOSITION

Composition is the conscious arrangement of the plastic values within a given space, as a canvas or paper, etc. Design is another term for the same. The greatest aesthetic strength of a work is usually attributed to the composition. If line, color, texture, pattern, and form are the divisions, then composition is the general in the army of aesthetics. Composition is the study of space division. It is the planning of intervals between occurrences. It is the setting of the stage for the optimum expression of the narrative.

DYNAMIC VS. STATIC

The word dynamic refers to the situation where motion is implied in a composition, and constantly holds the interest of the viewer. A static composition may be interesting enough, yet it does not incur the same excitement upon second and third viewing.

SYMMETRY VS. ASYMMETRY

Symmetrical compositions are usually static, yet can have a formal elegance. Asymmetrical compositions of the same subject usually hold more interest and allow the artist greater creativity in the organization of pictorial elements.

SCALE

The sense of scale suggests proportional relationships between objects. Rocks, clouds, sand dunes, and waves are fractiles, shapes in nature that need human attributes to give them scale. Figure 5 illustrates this point by showing a similar rock in each sketch, in combination with two differing human attributes; in turn, each sketch presents the viewer with a completely different sense of scale.

Figure 5: These pictures illustrate scale by showing a similar rock in each sketch, in combination with two differing human attributes; in turn, each sketch presents the viewer with a completely different sense of scale.

The Terminology of Color of the Color Wheel

The Primary Colors – red, yellow, blue (figure 6, page 97 – double line triangle)
In pigment mixtures, these colors are called primary because they cannot be obtained by mixtures of other colors. All other colors are obtained by mixtures of the primaries.

The Secondary Colors – orange, green, violet (figure 6, page 97– single line triangle) are obtained by mixtures of adjacent primaries.

The Tertiary Colors – yellow orange, yellow green, blue green, blue violet, red violet, red orange are obtained by mixtures of adjacent primaries and secondaries.

Complimentary Colors – colors that are opposite on the color wheel (figure 6, page 97 – connected by straight dotted lines); complimentary colors when placed next to each other produce strongest contrast.

Tint, Tone, and Shade – A *tint* is a mixture of pure color with white.
A *tone* is a mixture of pure color with gray or its complement.
A *shade* is a mixture of pure color with black.

Hue is the term used for the family of color as found on the color wheel.

Chroma is the strength or brightness of a hue. Example: Pthalo green has greater chroma than earth green.

How Three Illustrators Work

It is interesting and helpful to note how very differently illustrators work. There is no correct way to illustrate, and your way can draw its strength from being unique. The following three case histories for this chapter are more detailed and expanded than those in the rest of the book. They are, as much as possible, demonstrations of actual book projects written by illustrator Emily Arnold McCully, Caldecott Medalist in 1992; Jean Cassels, illustrator of numerous nonfiction picture books; and Berthe Amoss, illustrator of picture books and author of this book.

Emily Arnold McCully

As I always remind school audiences, I am an illustrator, not an artist. Every picture is composed to serve a text, or narrative, and therefore I know in my head at the outset how I want it to turn out (whether or not I succeed). An "artist," in my view, is an explorer who embarks without an end in mind.

Given this clear goal, I still try foremost for a look of liveliness and spontaneity in the work (figures 21, 22, and 23 on page 103). Readers must be able to enter into pictures for them to work as narrative elements. A gorgeous surface can be

forbidding. I keep my sketches loose until the very last minute, submitting dummies that require a lot of imagination to interpret. I never use color until the finish stage, so that there remain a great many problems to solve. I hope that the energy it takes to solve them will invigorate the painting.

I am most interested in characterization and action — characters doing things that help to reveal them and give the pictures dramatic power. It's like making up a movie. I seldom use models, so the effort is to translate what's in my head to the page. This is always more or less agony. Often, I will redo a picture many times just to get a small face right. Very seldom does the paint perform some unexpected miracle on its own. This did happen in a recent book set in Ireland, where watercolor naturally helped create misty seascapes, to my delight.

I am setting books more often in the past. I research costumes and settings in library books and the Picture Collection, a quaint enclave in the New York Public Library, which houses thousands of clipped photographs from various sources. I am very impatient with this sort of thing, since my penchant is for the scrawled line drawing. But having to pay attention to details and get them right has improved my work. I have noticed that many artists seem to "do things the hard way," working against their natural instincts or even abilities, and I am certainly one of them.

Every story is different and calls for different sorts of illustrations. Over the years, my style has never been fixed, because of this, I don't usually plan on a palette, but it seems to emerge differently every time, even though I rely mostly on a limited set of dry watercolors of the sort children use. This has been supplemented lately by tubes and pastels. I purchased the latter singly and without anything in mind, so their range is also an accidental determinant. It used to be that color and depth were lost in printing, but technology has improved. Still, original art still looks much more alive than the books.

JEAN CASSELS

All assignments begin with a call from my agent. She discusses with me the company, designs, schedule, and budget. Once we've agreed, she will send me a job order and contract.

Depending on the nature of the assignment, storybook, textbook, or part of a larger reading program, the instructions from the art director will be more or less specific. On this project, *Prairie Dogs*, I was given nearly 100 per cent artistic control. I received page layouts with the manuscript in place, but I was able to rearrange it as needed to best design the page with my art.

To begin, I read the manuscript, looked at the page layouts, and then did thumbnail sketches of each page for the entire book. This overview of the book helps to get a good balance of light, dark, colorful, quiet, up-close view, far-away view, action, calm, left-to-right movement, right-to-left movement, heavy on top, or heavy on the bottom.

When doing the actual sketches, I kept a notebook to record my references for each page. Next to the manuscript page number, I wrote what the reference was for — plants in background or paws of prairie dog — then I recorded the reference information — book title and page or scrap or personal photo. This saved me time and frustration when going back to do the finishes. I recommend maintaining a clip file, collecting books, and taking lots of photos.

For *Prairie Dogs*, I spent many hours at the Audubon Zoo observing, sketching, and taking photos of prairie dogs. This was an invaluable experience, helping me to understand their posture, movements, and interactions.

After completing the sketches, I made copies of each one. The sketches went to the designer at Scholastic with their page layouts.

When the sketches are returned, I'm always hoping to see: Good! Great! But sometimes there will be comments, or suggestions or requests for changes — sometimes small, sometimes large — even needing new sketches. At this point, you can discuss with the client and their consultant why you did what you did, using the reference that you had. If you've done your research well and explain your sketch and ideas well, perhaps they will let it stand. Otherwise you will have to make the changes. The point to remember in all of this is not egos but to make the best book possible.

My sketches are done in pencil on graphics 360, 100 per cent rag translucent marker paper. The finished work is done on 140-lb. hot-press Arches watercolor paper in gouache. Before beginning the finishes, I check my sketches against the reference and tighten up the sketches, making any changes I feel are necessary or to follow their comments for changes (figure 24, page 104).

I attach the sketch to the back of the watercolor paper, and working on a light box, I outline carefully the drawing, still working from my reference as well as the sketch.

I check my thumbnail sketch for colors and do a larger color sketch; then I mix my colors to begin the painting.

I lay in large washes, and working carefully, I go from the general to the specific (figure 25, page 104). On this book, *Prairie Dogs*, the very last thing to do was prairie-dog whiskers!

Before sending the finishes off to the client, I check each painting for any last touch-ups (figure 26, page 104). I clean up any smudges or fingerprints on the margins and erase all unnecessary pencil lines. I have to be certain that the corrected page number is written on each painting, along with the job number, job name, my name, and my agent's name.

Parchment is attached to each painting to protect it, and all the paintings are put together between heavy cardboard, with a cover letter to the designer stating what I'm sending and which book it is for.

BERTHE AMOSS

I read and loved the classic nursery tales and fairy tales as a child, but I fell in love with them when I taught children's literature. The stories provide so many levels of satisfaction and evoke visual images, which beg to be illustrated. And, of course, the classic tales are in the public domain, fair game for any writer or illustrator to interpret or twist.

I chose "The Gingerbread Boy" because I remembered loving the refrain "Run, Run, fast as you can! You can't catch me, I'm the Gingerbread Man!" I also remembered being upset over the ending, "And that was the end of the gingerbread man." I wanted to change the ending without damaging the integrity of the tale. I also wanted to do a book that was half toy and could be played with as well as read.

I made a book dummy to show my editor with a separate, paper doll Gingerbread Boy traveling through slit pages of Louisiana landscapes. I secured the paper doll to the cover with a cookie cutter and wrote a recipe on the back to resurrect him.

The Cajun Gingerbread Boy was born, and growing with it, as in all picture books, were its own, unique set of problems and solutions involving many people and changes.

My editor, Elizabeth Gordon, eliminated the cookie cutter as superfluous (thank goodness — what a packaging nightmare that would have been!) and asked me to "cajunize" the text. The wolf in the story immediately turned into an alligator, and the text was adapted with the help of Cajun cousins and Coleen Salley, professor of Children's Literature at the University of New Orleans and a master Cajun storyteller.

The cover presented the biggest problem. We had to secure the paper doll and get the slit-page concept across to the reader while the book was still shrink-wrapped.

In the cajunizing process, I had gone to great pains to make the alligator look realistic, studying alligators at the zoo, in the bayous, and, of course, in *National Geographic* magazine.

I hand-printed the title in letters made to look like gingerbread (figure 11, page 99), but before the cover got to the printer, Ellen Friedman, the art director, changed my letters to far more legible ones in red.

The slit jaws holding the gingerbread boy worked fine until the book went into production. At that point, in order to make the gingerbread boy fit into the jaws, the printer had to duplicate the alligator and paste him on top of the original one (figure 12). The alligator on the original cover could be seen behind the pasted one, and the cut-off body of the alligator ended abruptly too close to the spine. The cover looked sloppy. At the eleventh hour, I redid the whole cover making two paintings: the background and a separate alligator with water hyacinths to camouflage the trouble spot near the spine (figure 13).

By the time the cover was finalized, the realistic alligator in his natural habitat, at the zoo, and in *National Geographic* photos had turned into a caricature, M'sieur Cocodrie.

Now *The Cajun Gingerbread Boy* is out in its tenth anniversary edition.

For some unhappy reason, I almost always have to do all of my "final" illustrations twice. I call the second run my "finalies."

In one of the *Gingerbread Boy* illustrations, I was just about to put the last touch of paint to paper when my husband, looking over my shoulder, said, "That shrimper is rowing! You'll be the laughingstock of every Cajun fisherman in Louisiana — you paddle a pirogue!" I started over.

66

Chapter 7

SENDING IT OFF, SUBMITTING A MANUSCRIPT

A writer needs to know where to send his story. Which publisher will like it? Nowadays, knowing where to send your manuscript is harder than ever. Many publishers publicize the fact that they do not read unsolicited submissions, or submissions from authors unrepresented by agents, or manuscripts in certain genres. Persistent writers can still break down these barriers. But the barriers seem higher and more forbidding than ever.

If you are working on children's books, tell people what you are doing. Communicating with the people you know and networking can be important ways of identifying potential homes for your work. One writer told her husband about her story. He told a colleague at his law firm. The colleague had recently represented a publishing company. The writer sent her story to the publisher and sold her work the first time out. Now many of the companies that still exist have merged or been acquired, with the result that there are a few very large children's-book publishers. Vestiges of the component companies' original personalities remain. But the fact is that where you used to be able to submit work to both Harper & Row and William Morrow, those two companies have been subsumed into HarperCollins. Thus, opportunities for writers have been halved.

In theory, however, each formerly independent company operates as an imprint of the larger company. Think of a department store: In Bloomingdales, there is a counter for Chanel cosmetics and a counter for Estée Lauder cosmetics. So, in Penguin Putnam, for instance, there are Viking children's books and Grosset & Dunlap children's books. Though part of the same company, each imprint retains a unique identity as well as a separate editorial staff. To some extent, the exercise for the

TALK TO STRANGERS (BERTHE)

I wrote and illustrated two picture books for Ursula Nordstrom, but when I showed her my third, a wordless story called *By the Sea*, she said she had one wordless story on her list already. I took *By the Sea* to Susan Hirschman. She turned it down nicely: "I'm sure someone will publish it," she said. "Who?" I asked, and she gave me five publisher's names.In the lobby of Macmillan's office building, there was a line of public telephone booths, separated by low walls. I went into one and called Viking, the first name on Susan's list. I was told to send my manuscript in like everyone else. "But I'm only in New York today!" I said."I couldn't help hearing you," said a woman in the next booth after I'd hung up. "Why don't you try Alvin Tresselt at Parents? I used to work for him and he's very nice."I dialed the number and got an appointment. Alvin took *By the Sea* and subsequently five more books, but who was the woman in the telephone booth? All I could tell the people I came to know and like at Parents was that she was a curly-headed blonde in a large coat. They were puzzled, but I always thought she was my guardian angel.

aspiring writer remains the same: identifying imprints that seem most likely to publish books like the one you want to submit.

Be warned, however, that all the imprints may report to the same corporate publishing board, the group of decision-makers who choose what gets published. Thus, if you submit a manuscript to Viking that gets rejected by the board, resubmitting it to Grosset & Dunlap only means that the board will recognize a work they already jettisoned. Most likely, they may have the same response again. On the plus side, the board members may reject a story for the Viking list but ask the Grosset & Dunlap editors to consider it for inclusion on their list. The two imprints retain distinctive identities.

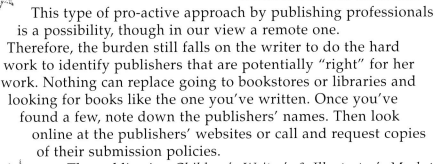

This type of pro-active approach by publishing professionals is a possibility, though in our view a remote one. Therefore, the burden still falls on the writer to do the hard work to identify publishers that are potentially "right" for her work. Nothing can replace going to bookstores or libraries and looking for books like the one you've written. Once you've found a few, note down the publishers' names. Then look online at the publishers' websites or call and request copies of their submission policies.

The publication *Children's Writer's & Illustrator's Market* contains good information about publishers' areas of specialization, names of key personnel, addresses and telephone numbers, and may include other important facts, such as submission policies. A submission should always be addressed to a particular editor. Her name should be spelled correctly, and her title should be current. You can confirm this information by telephone. Publishing is a transient business, with frequent changes in editorial staff. If you don't feel like shelling out for a costly subscription to *Publishers Weekly*, the best way to keep track of who and where editors are is through a website at www.underdown.org, which lists personnel changes in the industry. (Bookmark this site!) This is also good information because editors moving to new posts often have immediate needs for new books; opportunity may attend moves you note in the trade. Another essential source of publisher information is the website of the Children's Book Council at www.cbcbooks.org/html/pubfaqs.html. The Society of Children's

Book Writers and Illustrators also makes useful information (and updates) available to its members. (You can find membership information online at www.scbwi.org.)

"It's a neat idea for a book, Mr. James, but there's way too many big words."

Something else has happened in children's books that makes today's landscape very different from what it used to be: agents. Years ago, it was the exceptional children's-book author who was represented by an agent. An agent is compensated by taking a percentage of the author's earnings for a book the agent places successfully with a publisher. The advances for children's books and rate of royalty earnings were just not impressive enough to interest most agents.

Now many publishers announce that they will not read manuscripts by authors who are not represented by agents. In our view, this is a somewhat nonsensical approach to the task of finding worthwhile manuscripts. If you want to find the best of the best, you must cast your net wide. The thrill of being an acquisitions editor is finding that first story by an unknown that can be turned into a successful book. Commercial reality today dictates that acquisitions editors function much less as arbiters of taste and literary quality than as marketing mavens. The hard work of finding talent and developing salable stories is now done by agents. Agents who specialize in representing children's authors tend to make up in volume what

SMALL WORLD (ERIC)

In my first law job in New York, I found myself working for a senior partner whose daughter just happened to be a top editor at a major children's-book publishing company. While I worked for this partner, I never felt quite right about contacting the daughter about my writing. After all, I was in his office to work as a lawyer, and it seemed best not to mix my two professions. After I left the firm, though, a publishing friend mentioned this editor to me as someone with whom she enjoyed working. I contacted the editor, presented my credentials, and we had a pleasant chat. Then she said, "Can I ask you a funny question?" "Sure," I replied. "Did you used to work for my dad?" I've since done two major projects for that publisher. Who knows which contact did the trick?

You Know People (Eric)

I was giving a talk about writing for children at a big bookstore in Manhattan. One attendee was someone I knew as a professional writer, thought not as a writer for children. She admitted that she was only now completing her first work for children. She had come to the event specifically to ask for my recommendations about where to send it. We got to talking about celebrities in children's-book publishing, and I mentioned that Julie Andrews had just started her own imprint at HarperCollins. "I knew that," the writer said. "You did?" I asked. "I know Julie," said the writer. In addition to her other activities, this writer was a script doctor who had worked on Ms. Andrews' Broadway play *Victor/Victoria.* "Wait a minute," I said. "You know Julie Andrews and where she is and how to get in touch with her and you're here asking me where to send your manuscript?" I find that people often don't think of obvious contacts they have in their chosen field. You may not know Julie Andrews; but if you think hard about everyone you do know, you will very likely be able to identify one or two contacts to the publishing world.

they miss in sizeable advances and fast-earning royalties. That is, the pay scale for authors has not increased much, so agents must work hard and place a lot of books to make the agency a worthwhile venture.

There are pros and cons to retaining an agent. The pluses include the agent's specialized knowledge of publishers and their needs and his familiarity with industry practices. For instance, an agent will know when a publisher is launching a new imprint aimed at toddlers and will get your story about play school to the appropriate editor more promptly than you could.

The drawbacks include the agent's cut of your earnings (the present industry standard is 15 percent for writers) and the fact that you may find yourself in competition with other authors he represents. Say that you have written a book about dinosaurs and so has another author represented by the same agent. The agent will not submit both stories to an editor interested in the dinosaur books. Rather the agent, may send the manuscript he likes best or the one by the author whose name can fetch the bigger advance.

If you retain an agent, he or she will handle all your submissions. But you must endure a similar submission process to find an agent. Seeking an agent is very much like seeking a publisher. Agents are listed in *Children's Writer's & Illustrator's Market.*

There are pros and cons to retaining an agent. The pluses include the agent's specialized knowledge of publishers and their needs and his familiarity with industry practices. An agent may also supply a buffer between the author and editor, allowing the creative relationship to flourish with the intrusion of worldly matters like money and contractual terms.

The manuscript should be presentable before you send it. It should be carefully typed and double-spaced. As you type, check the spelling and usage of each word. Check your punctuation. Neatness is not as vital in a book dummy. But a dummy should always be accompanied by a cleanly typed manuscript. If you have a good agent, she will not want to show a publisher anything but your best, most carefully written work.

When you review publishers' submission policies, you will note that some require query letters before submission. A query letter describes your story, its intended audience, its theme and format. It also introduces you and your special background to the editor. If your letter piques an editor's interest, she may invite you to submit the full manuscript. (One distinguished publisher I know used to say query letters were a waste of time for picture books, since generally it took just as much time to read the complete manuscript as to read the query letter. That's one reason why knowing a publisher's submission policies may help you-it may actually save you time and work.)

Your letter should also suggest the "flavor" of your manuscript. Be careful, however. A whimsical tone may help set the mood for your original fairy tale; a letter in verse may give a taste of your rhyming text. But a query letter is still essentially a business letter, and it must contain some strictly business information: the length and genre of your story, your target age group, whether illustrations are needed, the "message" you hope to send young readers, your commercial "hook," and your reasons for writing to this publisher. The "hook" is some commercially appealing factor that tells the editor your book will sell. (See Chapter 9 for more on hooks.)

You should also describe your actual experience with children. Trumpet your work as a teacher, counselor, or day-care worker. Any education you've had in writing for children — courses, workshops, seminars, group memberships — demonstrate commitment and some knowledge. Stress any prior publication of your writing — local magazines, trade or professional journals, campus newspapers. Any prior publication increases your credibility with publishers by letting them know that someone before them has liked your writing well enough to publish it. Experience as a parent or grandparent is common but worth mentioning. Keep your letter brief and to the point — two or three short paragraphs should suffice. If you feel you must write a longer letter, try not to exceed one page.

Here are two things not to say in your letter to publishers:

"I wrote the story for my children/grandchildren, and when I read it to them, they just loved it." Publishers justifiably feel that any child would love the experience of being held close by a beloved adult and read a story that was written just for him — this kind of puffery shows

---

EXERCISE

After you have finished your manuscript, write out a query letter "selling" it to a publisher.

- Describe your "idea": This portion should convey the commercial "hook," such as, "I have written a story about dinosaurs and divorce."

- Summarize the plot, briefly: "When Andy's parents divorce, he finds comfort in adventures with his imaginary dinosaur friend."

- Emphasize your theme: "This story emphasizes the power of imagination to help children cope with real-life situations."

- Define the genre, format, and age group: "This story, intended for readers in the grades K-2, is written in an easy-to-read style. It would be ideal in a softcover "I Can Read" format, 48 pages, with full-color illustrations."

- Describe yourself: "I am a teacher with ten years' experience introducing first and second graders to the fundamentals of reading."

A Primer on the Standard Publishing Contract

Most publishing contracts contain standard terms that are conceptually easy to understand though written in tangled English. Here is a summary of the basic provisions:

1) The author, the publisher and the work are identified; deadlines for your delivery of the work and its publication will also be included;

2) Warranty and Indemnity: You assure the publisher that the work is original with you; if this turns out not to be true, you agree to pay back any amount the publisher must pay the person whose copyright you infringed; you may also have to warrant that you will not attempt to have a "competing work" (e.g., a work on the same subject) published for a period of time after publication of the work under contract;

3) Copyright: The publisher agrees to register the work with the Copyright Office in your name. For this reason, do NOT copyright the work before submitting it;

4) Grant of Rights: You grant the publisher certain rights to the work under the copyright law – for instance, the right to print and distribute copies of the work, the right to make or authorize adaptations, the right to include the work in anthologies;

5) Royalty: The publisher agrees to pay you a specified royalty rate for use of each of the rights you grant it; the contract should also provide that you receive some advance to be held against future royalties, and that you have the right to audit the publisher's books as they pertain to your work;

6) Out-of-print: If the publisher ceases to publish the book, the contract can be terminated and all your rights returned to you (you may also be able to buy copies of the book or printing materials at a reduced price from the publisher's remaining stock).

Publishing contracts typically run to five or ten pages or more, so there are many provisions beyond those listed above. However, this outline provides you with a basic primer on the nuts and bolts of what the contract tries to accomplish.

your qualities as a caregiver more than it demonstrates the quality of your writing.

"If you like this story, I have a whole series based on the same characters/theme/idea." Publishers find this notion frightening. They need to like one story first, and you're putting the cart before the horse by trying to sell the others before the first has a home. Publishers may also think that your expectations are unrealistic and that you won't be satisfied with the publication of just one of your stories. Your first submission needs to stand alone. This is true despite the fact that generally a publisher wants to find a writer who will be good for more than one book.

Many manuscripts go astray when they are submitted "over the transom," that is, without a prior query and without a green light from an editor. Merely adding an editor's name to the outside of the envelope will not necessarily solve your problem; publishers have procedures for tracking which manuscripts they've asked to see. Even with an editor's name, an unsolicited manuscript may end up on the stack of manuscripts processed by the company's "slush" readers. These readers plow through the work of hopeful writers who have not researched the company's submission policies. Often, slush readers can give manuscripts little more than a cursory glance.

The "slush" readers are the people who most likely will evaluate your query letter and manuscript, so you should know something about your first "audience." These readers are often entry-level workers called editorial assistants. They are usually young, college-educated people with a love of books and the ambition to move into positions as editors. They want the opportunity to discover and develop writers of "their own," for that is the best way for them to demonstrate their ability and move ahead in their careers. Even solicited manuscripts are most often read by these eager people, who are hired to do all the "drudge" work their busy bosses lack time to do.

For an editorial assistant, reading manuscripts is just one of many tasks. Other duties include answering phones, typing letters and manuscripts, proofreading and trafficking galleys, checking sketches, final artwork, and proofs, and writing reports on projects the boss has already signed up. The time-consuming process of reading and evaluating manuscripts with only a slight chance of acceptance seems unrewarding and unimportant. Still, the higher-ups often emphasize the importance of this work, and the fear of passing up a diamond among the dross is palpable and provides incentive. A top editor used to allay assistants' fear of missing a gem by saying, "Don't worry; if it's really good, someone will publish it." And the law of averages suggests that she was right.

Thus, these readers, like most editors, want to find something publishable in the slush pile. You can make an overwhelmed reader sit up and take notice in two ways: through the quality of your work, and through the professionalism of your presentation. Spelling every word in your letter and manuscript correctly and putting the correct punctuation in the right places are rarer accomplishments than you might think. They make reading your work that much easier and more pleasant, and make you appear that much more credible as a candidate for furthering the literacy of young people.

NETWORKING OPPORTUNITIES

Here are great places to meet children's-book professionals:

- Writers' conferences (many cities, universities, and organizations have them; check the programs for sessions on children's books)

- Writing courses (check the course catalog for the instructor's credentials; also chat up your fellow students, who may have more credentials or contacts than you realize)

- Author appearances at local bookstores (authors on autographing tours are often accompanied by editors, art directors, or others from their publishers' offices)

- Author talks sponsored by writers' groups (chapters of the Society of Children's Book Writers and Illustrators often feature guest speakers at meetings)

Publishers used to frown on simultaneous submissions, which means submitting the same work to more than one publisher at a time. Publishers wanted to be sure they were being offered properties exclusively before they went to the time and expense of reviewing the manuscripts and forming business plans. Nowadays, most publishers are prepared to see simultaneous submissions. However, you should inform the publisher that you are submitting your manuscript simultaneously at the time of your first communication.

The submission process may take a long time. Publishers try to control how long they hold manuscripts before responding. Give the publisher about six weeks before you start following up. Don't be angry or threatening when you communicate with a publisher at this stage — that is a sure way to get a speedy rejection, regardless of the quality of your work. And always include a self-addressed, stamped envelope with your submission.

Some publishers have the courtesy to send each author a postcard stating that the publisher has received the manuscript, but many publishers do not. Consider enclosing a self-addressed, stamped postcard with your manuscript. Type something on the postcard to the effect that "We have received your manuscript and will be back in touch after we have completed our review." You may wish to leave a blank space where the editor can sign, or a box for her to check. But make it easy for the editor simply to pull the postcard out of your envelope and place it in her "out" box to be returned to you.

Remember, this is a business letter and should have a businesslike tone. Do not start your letter with the word "I"; emphasize the publisher's needs. For example: "Your series of easy-to-read books for first and second graders has been a boon to me and other teachers of my acquaintance. Now I have written a manuscript that you may wish to consider for inclusion in this series." Reread your letter. How could you describe your story better? Reread your story. How could you rewrite it to be more appealing?

Chapter 8

REJECTION AND REVISION

---

*B*y mailing or e-mailing your manuscript to the publisher, you kick-start the entire decision-making apparatus of the company. What happens to your book after it is submitted? It is the great paradox of children's publishing that although children must like your book if it is to become a classic, they don't have any say in getting it published. Adult editors have to like your book. Adult editors are sometimes asked whether they "use" children in their decision-making. The answer, for the most part, is no. Very occasionally, a publisher may invest in focus-group testing, where panels of children are exposed to the new book "product," observed and questioned about it. The process is costly, and publishers only use it when they are committing to a major, very visible project with a huge commitment of resources at risk.

The reason why children do not participate in the decision-making reflects a commercial reality: Children do not buy children's books nor, with a few notable exceptions, do they review or give awards for children's books. Responsible educators and parents who want to know that trained professionals are screening children's books for literary quality and age-appropriate content. Publishing companies want to know that the same professionals are screening submissions with an eye to commercial values.

It's a great start if one editor likes your story, though that may not be enough to make the publisher issue a contract. After forming a favorable impression of your work, the editor has to take the story of "editorial meeting" and get the other members of the editorial staff "on board." This process may involve detailed evaluation by other editors on the staff. He has to persuade the art director to try to give the book the right "look." If there is a novel format, he must work with the production department to make sure the special feature can be done cost-effectively. He must prepare a publishing proposal including a projected profit-and-loss statement showing cost factors, expected sales based on the performance of similar books in the marketplace.

He has to persuade his superiors on the publishing board that the book demonstrates high quality and makes sense for the publisher's list. In today's world, with few decision-makers considering myriad literary properties, that may mean using shorthand that conveys the story's appeal: "Think Harry Potter with a Lemony Snicket twist." Or: "It's like that book by Madonna, but if she could write." That's why giving your story a "hook" that can be expressed in few words (see Chapter 9) can be so important to its success.

The sales and marketing forces will weigh in. The sales executives may say they can sell your board-book-and-CD package, but only if the price is under $12.95. Now the editor may have to rework the proposal to exclude cost factors that would drive the retail price above that point. These compromises may impact your vision of the book but may be necessary to make the book commercially viable. The marketing people will ask whether the book is promotable. Again, this is where your "hook" comes in. Your personal background and qualifications may become important, too. Let's say you've been involved with particular community groups or school groups. Are there any special events that present opportunities to sell books to those groups?

Once the package is all together, but before publication, the editor must sell the book to the sales force at large. A sales conference is often held close to publication, and the fortune of a book can rise or fall based on the sales staff's responses.

Rejection letters may be written by the editor at any of several stages in the process-after a first reading, after an editorial meeting, after a profit-and-loss analysis shows that the book would not generate sufficient revenue to offset the cost and earn a profit. But what does it mean when you receive a rejection?

Most often it means that some editor did not like your book. Or it may not mean anything as definite as that. It may mean that your book didn't "hit" the editor, didn't suddenly leap up as something he should spend time advocating or the company should go out of its way to produce. It doesn't mean your book is in some sense "bad." You have to learn to pick yourself up and start again. Send your manuscript to another house right away.

DEAR MS. POTTER,

THANK YOU FOR SENDING US YOUR MANUSCRIPT. UNFORTUNATELY WE DO NOT HAVE A PLACE ON OUR LIST FOR A SMALL BOOK ABOUT A NAUGHTY BUNNY.

HOWEVER, YOU WRITE RATHER WELL, AND ALTHOUGH, OF COURSE, WE CAN'T PROMISE ANYTHING, WE WONDER IF YOU MIGHT TRY YOUR HAND AT A TALE ABOUT BABY DINOSAURS.

SINCERELY YOURS,
a Blatherac, P.H.E.W.
PUBLISHER

Remember that in submitting your story, you are placing yourself in competition with some formidable rivals for publishers' dollars. Your story must be extra distinctive and extra good because a publisher will be asking whether its money is better spent paying an advance to an unknown author rather than taking out a few more ads for a pop star's children's book in which the publisher already has a huge investment. Do whatever you can to give your book something a publisher feels it can't live without.

But keep in mind that once you've done so, there is no shame in losing out to Madonna. That's the reality of today's marketplace.

What is a rejection letter? Generally, it is a form letter that you receive in response to your query or as a cover letter with your returned manuscript. It will usually employ some cryptic and frustrating phrases in a lame attempt to explain why the publisher has chosen not to publish your story. However, you should know that publishers often use these time-honored formulations for a beneficent purpose-they don't want you to waste time altering your story in response to specific criticism when the manuscript may be just right for some other publisher.

That rationale holds if your story has any merit. An editor experiences a rare sinking feeling when reading a manuscript with not a single redeemed feature. In such a circumstance, an editor is very happy to have these stock phrases to coin anew. But don't assume that your manuscript falls into this category just because these old bromides appear in the letter you receive.

Be Persistent (Berthe)

After four years of rejections, I finally "recognized" a good idea when my three-year-old had a temper tantrum because his nine-year-old brother had a birthday. I was about to go to New York, so I wrote Susan Hirschman at Harper & Row, to whom I had been submitting picture-book manuscripts, asking for an appointment.

Charlotte Zolotow wrote back that Susan was no longer with them but that they would see me at eleven o'clock the day I requested.

Through sheer serendipity with some magic thrown in, I happened to see an announcement in *Publishers Weekly*, a magazine I didn't know existed, that Susan was at Macmillan. I wrote to her, and she gave me an appointment at ten o'clock the day I requested.

When she saw it, Susan liked my story and made a note in the margin. But she didn't take it, and I went on to my eleven o'clock appointment at Harper & Row. Charlotte liked my story, too, and brought me and it to Ursula Nordstrom, the formidable editor-in-chief of Harper & Row.

In reading *It's Not Your Birthday*, Ursula noticed Susan's note. "Who wrote this? Are you free to offer us this manuscript?" she asked.

"Susan Carr (Hirschman later)," I answered. "Yes, I'm free."

"Then, we'll take it." Ursula said the magic words, but I have never known whether she took it because she loved it or because she was angry that Susan had left Harper.

You can read several morals into this case history as I see it, but the most important is that persistence pays off. Second, the most marketable aspect of a picture book text is the uniqueness of your heartfelt idea behind it.

Try not to put too much pressure on the editor, or yourself, at the review stage. It may be just a waste of time and resources and merely serve to delay the inevitable rejection. For instance, don't travel long distances to meet with an editor to whom you're submitting work for the first time. If the editor doesn't like your work, the travel will make her feel more guilty about rejecting your work but will not influence her to like it if she doesn't like it already. Don't make an editor sign a confidentiality agreement before giving them your work to consider. Doing so will

TRY, TRY AGAIN! (ERIC)

A no from a particular publisher does not have to be forever. When I was still an editorial assistant, a rising illustrator submitted a picture book dummy that I loved. This story about a family of performing bears was a perfect fit with my theatrical background. At the editorial meeting, the consensus was that the project was "not for us." Just a few years later, I had progressed from an assistant with no power to a full editor with control of my own list of books. When presented with the challenge of developing a series of books that would be truly "special," I set about soliciting the work of writers and artists whom I admired. One of these was Emily Arnold McCully. Emily sent in the story about the performing bears, which I easily recognized from years before. Now I could act on my desires, and I jumped to get *The Show Must Go On* for my list. (See page 93 for her essay.)

make an editor suspect you are litigious or at least have an exaggerated sense of the originality of your work and will probably hasten a rejection. If you get an in-person appointment with an editor, make your pitch and leave your work for the editor's leisurely review. Do not make the editor review your work while you sit looking on from the visitor's chair. Editors, like many people, don't like confrontation and in any event prefer to express themselves in writing. They may find it difficult to tell you to your face that they dislike your work, and therefore may ask to keep it for another reading.

They may find it difficult to like your work because you're sitting there pressuring them to do so. Letting the editor relax with your work, by himself, may be the best way to get the most positive response.

All that a rejection letter really means, then, is that a particular editor on a particular day did not like your manuscript. Editors have only a few qualifications for their jobs — one is language skills; but the other more important requirement is taste. An editor does not have to have good taste to be a good editor — she merely has to have taste that reflects the aesthetic of her company and some segment of the buying public. Thus, the editor who published the American edition of *Everyone Poops* by Taro Gomi recognized that small children like bathroom humor, that some parents pander to their children's baser preferences, and that her company could successfully market such a book. It wasn't an exercise in good taste, but it worked for the company and for a segment of the buying public.

The following sample rejection letters summarize differing responses to the same manuscript. In other words, all rejec-

© Emily Arnold McCully

tion letters are not the same! Each of these letters calls for a different type of response.

> *Dear Author:*
>
> *Thank you for sending your manuscript,* Dolly's Busy Day, *which we have read with interest. While your story has merit, we regret that we do not have a place for it on our list at this time. Perhaps another publisher will have a different response.*
>
> *Your manuscript is returned herewith, with thanks for the opportunity to consider it.*
>
> *Sincerely,*
> *Ed Editor*

This is a form rejection letter. You can tell because it says nothing specific about you or your story besides your name and title. You should put this letter aside and move on. Now consider the following letter:

> *Dear Author:*
>
> *Thank you for sending your manuscript,* Dolly's Busy Day, *which we have read with interest. While the simple story is not quite right for our list, which is heavily weighted toward school-age children who can already read a little, we admired your tight plotting and sprightly dialogue. If you should ever decide to try your hand at a story in the easy-to-read genre, we would be most interested to see it.*
>
> *Your manuscript is returned herewith, with regret. Thank you for the opportunity to consider it.*
>
> *Sincerely,*
> *Ed Editor*

This letter is a "come-on." The editor clearly liked some very specific things about your writing and wants to see more. If you are not sure what the jargon means — for instance, the phrase "easy-to-read genre" — this is an opportunity to start a dialogue with the editor. Pick up the phone and call, or write a letter expressing your gratitude and interest in exploring possibilities on the editor's terms.

A less clear-cut situation may be presented by a letter such as the following:

> *Dear Author:*
>
> *Thank you for sending your manuscript,* Dolly's Busy Day, *which we have read with interest. This story is not right for our list in its present form, though we enjoyed your tight plotting and sprightly dialogue. The simplicity of your manuscript is one of its virtues but is not in keeping with the tone of our picture book list, which emphasizes stories that will lend themselves to lavish illustration by award-winning artists and top-notch production values. If Dolly were a Victorian porcelain doll rather than a homemade ragdoll, her story might work better for us, especially with a few more episodes providing an opportunity to show rich settings and period detail.*

If you should decide to rework your story along the lines mentioned above, we would be happy to take another look. Meantime, your manuscript is returned herewith, with thanks for the opportunity to consider it.

Sincerely,
Ed Editor

Now the author has a quandary. She wrote about a homemade ragdoll because she had such a doll when she was a girl and wanted to show children that humble things could be beautiful and lovable. She feels hurt because some big-city editor has rejected her Dolly. This writer may put the letter away and keep trying with the story in its present form.

But wait. There might be another approach. A story employing the suggested elements might imply your original theme by playing up the "bird in the gilded cage" aspects of the porcelain doll's existence. Of course, this approach would work only if the writer felt truly comfortable with the editor's ideas — merely writing to suit the editor may not work unless the author has a genuine response to the suggestion. In the end, the benefit may be that the writer has two manuscripts that work rather than one — the frilly doll story for the publisher who wants that approach, and the plain one for another publisher. (One caveat: The author may want to be careful about competing with herself; in fact, many publishing contracts contain a provision requiring that the author not publish another book with subject matter similar to the one under contract until a certain period of time has passed. The author may also want to be wary about being typecast as the person who writes the doll stories.)

The lesson to be learned here is to read your rejection letters. Ordinarily, they will be of the form type typified by sample number one above, and you may not feel that the publisher has even read your story. However, if the letter contains any specific criticism or reaction to your story, it may not be a complete rejection, as in samples two and three. A busy editor rarely takes time to make an individual comment on your work unless it aroused her interest.

An editor may ask you to revise "on spec." This phrase means that if you revise according to the editor's instructions and he is satisfied with your changes, your story may be accepted for

BE TRUE TO YOUR TALE (ERIC)

If you cannot live with the editor's vision of your work, say so. You will save a lot of heartache and needless work. I once received a manuscript about a talking Christmas tree — not my sort of thing at all, and a shameless (and shamelessly sentimental) exploitation of Andersen's "The Little Fir Tree." Nevertheless, I saw commercial potential there. Problem: The author had written a novella, and I saw the story as a 24-page Little Golden Book. I kept asking the author to revise "on spec," but she didn't get what I was asking her to do. Finally, I did it myself to show her my idea. I trimmed the branches from her tree, so to speak, whittled the text until it fit neatly into the 24-page format. The author was dismayed to see a twig in place of her mighty fir and rejected my offer of a contract. The integrity of her vision was important to her, and she was right. She would never have been happy with the truncated tree.

EXERCISE

Editors-in-training must learn to trust their instinct that something is "wrong" when it sets off a bell in their heads. You can develop this instinct, too, and use it to revise effectively even without an editor's input. Go through your manuscript carefully. Identify each and every spot that sounds "not right" to you. Now work to fix each of those spots, making sure the changes are true to the theme and tone of your story.

publication. If your changes are not satisfactory and your book is not published, you will get nothing for your trouble. If you are revising on spec, be on your best behavior. The editor will be looking to see how you handle revisions. But he will also be interested in your attitude. Do you answer correspondence promptly? Are you cooperative? Are you willing to trust the editor? Can you articulate reasoned responses when you disagree? Publishing is a collaborative business. You should seem to be willing to work together to make a final product that will suit everyone's needs.

In today's publishing world, agents are the norm for children's-book authors. Many suggestions for revision may come from your agent or even from an agent who is only considering representing you. Traditionally, working with authors to polish and perfect their work was an editor's bread-and-butter. No more. Due to consolidation in publishing companies, fewer editors are in charge of many more books and have less time to devote to working with aspiring writers who may or may not pan out. They also have less time to work on perfecting and polishing books they are seriously considering or have acquired for publication. As a result, agents have come to serve much more of an editor's role. Persuading an agent to represent you is an investment in your future access to publishers, and you may want to think hard about and work seriously with an agent's suggestions. However, as we said in connection with editors, if an agent's vision is truly out of step with your view of your work, you may be better off trying to find one more in tune with your vision.

Revision, however, is a tricky business, and because you will seldom get two readers, professional or friends, who will agree, it is sometimes best not to revise until an editor has seen your original manuscript.

EXERCISE

If you have received a personalized rejection letter along the lines mentioned in this chapter, try to revise your story to meet the editor's objections. How do you feel about the result? Is it still "your" story? Would you be able to live with its being published under your name?

If you have not received such a rejection letter, share your story with a writers' group or a trusted, experienced, published friend. Assure your readers that you want them to be absolutely honest and to provide constructive advice. Don't be defensive when you get feedback — in fact, it may be better to have your readers provide written responses. Decide if you agree with any of the criticism you receive, and try to revise your story accordingly if after reflection you can see your story from another point of view.

EXERCISE

Go through your manuscript looking at every adjective and adverb in your text. Now try to eliminate as many as you can without losing meaning. You can do this by using powerful nouns and verbs, which will make your prose more concise and stronger. If you wrote "ran quickly," try "sped." If you wrote "big stone," try "boulder." Some adjectives, such as color words, cannot be replaced. But try to eliminate as many as you can.

EXERCISE

If you have written your story in verse, rewrite it in prose. Publishers dislike verse because it is very hard to tell a story in that format without sacrificing either clear meaning or smooth, consistent meter and rhyme. As you rewrite in prose, try to keep as much of the good word play and fun sounds from your verse as you can. Occasional rhyme is okay, especially at special places in the text that may function as a refrain of a certain type of dialogue (e.g., a riddle, a magic spell).

SELF-EDITING CHECKLIST

- Review your manuscript thoroughly.

- Make sure you are expressing yourself as clearly as possible.

- Make sure you are not using too many words; eliminate all unnecessary adverbs and adjectives.

- Break up complex sentence structures; one thought per sentence is a good rule of thumb.

- Make sure that each thought flows logically from the one before it.

- Eliminate redundancies.

- Look for incorrect or poor word choices and replace them with more effective and appropriate words.

- Check for places where adding dialogue or describing a character's sensations would make the prose more alive.

A Graphic Designer Discusses Her Work

Rebecca Blake

Every major publishing house has a graphic designer or art director. We have asked Rebecca Blake, our own designer and President of The Graphic Artists Guild of New York, to explain the important but little known role designers play in creating books for children. She has been a working designer since 1990 and is currently Design Director for Optimum Design and Consulting, a small firm in mid-town Manhattan.

I neither write nor illustrate children's books. I'm a graphic designer, a profession that isn't always clearly defined. Essentially, I put a "face" on a company, a product, or a publication.

Children's-book design is a unique category. Unlike other publications, children's-book design is a balancing act between three sometimes competing influences: the author, the illustrator, and the needs of the target audience. That last concern can trump the other two. For example, it doesn't matter how beautifully a read-along book is illustrated; if the text is too small for the child to manage, the book isn't reaching its audience. I've done just a few children's-book projects, but I've had extensive experience in publication design. In the best of situations I'll try to create a design that complements both the text and the images, picking a typeface that stylistically echoes the tone of the story, and creating a layout that shows off the artwork but makes the text legible for the reader.

Good design in children's books reflects good writing and good illustration; poor design can muddy a story. Of course I'm not saying that every writer or illustrator needs to take design classes, but you should look at classic children's books, and pay attention to the typography and layout. Notice the typeface, even if you don't know its name. Think of what it "feels" like: Is it bold, or flowery, or old fashioned? Pay attention to the layout. Is the text in one lump, or spread across the page? Does it make a rectangular box, with straight edges on both sides, or is it ragged on one side? Did the designer play with the typography, stretching the letters, or making the words bounce, or scattering the letters of individual words?

When creating your book dummy, try to consider some of these ideas. Bear in mind that your book publisher will have a lot of input into how the book is structured — and may just shoot down your design ideas. But even in that instance, thinking about the design of your book is going to reinforce your thinking about the book as a whole, rather than as a series of pretty pictures and a nice story. When you think about your book's typography, you're really thinking about the mood you're setting for the book. And when you think about your book's layout — where and how the words will fall — you're really thinking about your book's pacing and rhythm. The goal of a designer is to create a strong, unified visual identity for a book. Adopting some of those thought processes will make you a better writer and illustrator.

Chapter 9

EDITORS AND AGENTS AND WHAT THEY LOOK FOR

For aspirants hoping to break into print, editors' offices have always felt like castle keeps in old tales of chivalry. To get in, one had to slay dragons, swim moats, scale tall towers. This vision may contain more truth today than ever before. As we've mentioned throughout the book, there are fewer big publishers and fewer editors than there were in the past. Due to changes in the children's-book market and in the publishing industry, editors have less time to search for new talent. In today's children's-book market, "new talent" often seems to mean celebrities like Madonna or adult authors like Dean Koontz, who are "new" only in the sense that they have never before written for children.

In addition, many editors are cut off from the search for new talent by company policies requiring that submissions come only from agents.

So are editors looking only for celebrities and best-selling authors who've proven themselves in other genres? No! Editors are looking for the next Harry Potter, a literary property that is original, can spawn endless sequels and adaptations, and above all that can sell truckloads of books. But even more, editors are looking for the next J.K. Rowling-someone with the creativity and vision and sheer writing ability to build a world that is inviting for children and also adults. Remember that J.K. Rowling was an unknown at the beginning, that she struggled hard to write the first Harry Potter book and get it published. And look at her now.

Will editors stop short of the next Harry Potter in acquiring new titles? Yes! We continue to believe, based on the books that are published, that editors are primarily looking for talent. One of the greatest thrills of being an editor is discovering a talent whose work has never before been published. It doesn't take much talent to recognize that a book by Madonna or Dean Koontz will likely be a big seller. But an editor proves her mettle by being the first to discover someone unknown and truly special. The challenge for the children's-book writer is to mark himself as that special talent.

So what is talent? Talent is difficult to define but can reveal itself in many ways. Basically, it is the special ingredient you add that makes your book about dinosaurs different from all the others on the market. Talent may reveal itself in many different facets of your work. You may show talent by the way you narrow your subject. Let's say you're writing a book about dinosaurs. Choosing that tried-and-true topic shows no special talent. But maybe you've found a new slant on dinosaurs. If your book is nonfiction, you may have decided to write about a particular class or category of dinosaurs. If your story is fiction, perhaps you have chosen to use dinosaur characters for a good reason that relates to the theme of your story. If you're submitting a picture book, your story has a strong visual element that cries out for creative illustrations.

> ### MAKE THEM TALK
>
> Dialogue can be the thing that grabs a reader, including an editor, and makes the character and situation leap off the page. Look for the following lines in well-known books and read the surrounding scenes to see what makes them so special:
>
> "Seal was very worried!"
> (Chapter 9, *Sarah, Plain and Tall* by Patricia MacLachlan)
>
> "My-my hair!"
> (Chapter XV, *Little Women* by Louisa May Alcott)
>
> "Ugly as sin, calls herself Wilcox? . . . She's been in the state hospital for the insane until just here lately, but as a reporter I guess you nosed that out."
> ("Shotgun Cheatham's Last Night Above Ground," *A Long Way from Chicago* by Richard Peck)
>
> And in picture books:
>
> "Kiss me again," said Frances.
> (*Bedtime for Frances* by Russell Hoban)
>
> The entirety of *Yo! Yes?* by Chris Raschka

The most important talent, though, is a talent for good writing. Writing for children — like writing for anyone — is an art. It is difficult and takes time and requires that the artist build his skills into a technique. This book is an attempt to help you do so by identifying the issues and breaking down the elements of the task at hand. But the important contribution comes from you and your refusal to be satisfied with your work until every sentence feels alive.

Consider the difference between these two sentences:

"One sunny day, Mary walked down the street."

"Mary felt the sun on her face as she hurried to town."

Most editors — most readers — would rather read a story about a character who feels things and expresses a sense of purpose with her actions. The first sentence could be written by anyone with a PC; the second shows a talent for characterization and storytelling. However, good writing is not the only kind of talent that matters in writing for children. Judy Blume is an author whose writing shows a lot of rough edges and awkwardness. But Ms. Blume has an incomparable talent for accurately recognizing and depicting the true emotions of young people. Her stories may not be the most shapely, her prose not the most elegant, but her ability to penetrate the hearts and minds of young people is unique and has made her a popular and beloved author. Her being awarded the National Book Association's Medal for Distinguished Contribution to American Letters merely confirms what young readers have known for years.

Reading aloud is a good test of your writing. Many children's books are read aloud, so the "sound" of your work is important. Is your text lively, mellifluous, interesting when you say it? Don't be surprised to learn that picture-book editors test for these qualities by reading manuscripts aloud to themselves. It is a good sign if key phrases stick in the mind after the reader is finished. If you find yourself reciting little phrases out of context, you're probably succeeding. Keep in mind that children love to hear favorite stories again and again, and the memorable turn of phrase is one way to keep them wanting your story. Editors may have the same response.

A writer's talent for dialogue may be like an actor's talent for improvisation: Try to imagine things your character might say, and don't stop at the obvious. Your dialogue needs to do two things — reveal character and move the plot. Revealing character is where your talent can shine if you try to write dialogue that has individuality and charm.

Our hypothetical editor is also looking for a publishable manuscript, here defined as a well-written story with an interesting plot and a strong, universal theme. Like talent, plot is difficult to define; think of it as the thing that keeps the reader turning the pages. It is important that your story have all these features before you start sending it to editors. You can make sure by rereading it and analyzing it closely. Does it do all the things you want it to do? Does the action keep the reader turning the pages to find out what happens? Does the action clearly illustrate your underlying message? Don't write "for the market." Only by writing from your inspiration can you demonstrate the spark — the "talent" — that distinguishes your work.

Our hardworking editor is looking for one other ingredient in your manuscript—a "hook." A hook is a proven commercial element that can be exploited in marketing your book. (Marketing means promoting and selling.) A commercial hook may be a tried-and-true subject, like dinosaurs. It may be a special focus on that subject, for instance, baby dinosaurs. It may be some special expertise that you

Santa's Express, a die-cut Advent calendar book with windows children can open, combines several hooks.

© Berthe Amoss

86

can bring to the subject: Do you have access to new information about baby dinosaurs that has never been used in a children's book?

You can find your hook by visiting a library and looking at children's books on your subject. A survey will show you what books on the subject are being published and how your book differs from those on the market. If your book is not different or better, you may want to think about reworking it. If you don't want to rework your book, think about other ways to make it more marketable. Start with yourself: What degrees do you have, what experience, what background with the subject matter? Then think about the people you know — do you know a distinguished educator or scientist who would be willing to contribute a foreword to your book? You know those quotes by famous people on the covers of books you buy? Those quotes are solicited; the author or his agent or publisher approaches the famous people and asks them for quotable quotes that may be helpful in marketing the book. You can do the same for yourself at an earlier stage of the publishing process.

The fact is that a publisher may look at the people you know. The publishing world is like a small village in which most people know each other. Many authors are published because they know editors or other publishing professionals. People are published because they are related to well-known authors or illustrators or have a promise that such well-known people will somehow contribute to the book. At least one publisher asks prospective authors about their media contacts, in the interest of finding authors who can help promote their own books. The people you know may be your hook!

You need not be overly concerned if you don't have any hooks of this kind; just be aware that if you do have one, it may make publication an easier goal to reach. Editors are practiced in the art of identifying and exploiting the hook buried in the author's manuscript. But you have to hook the editor. Your talent may be

EXERCISE

Identify the hook in each of the following books. Remember that there may be more than one.

My Friend Rabbit by Eric Rohmann

A Year Down Yonder by Richard Peck

The Man Who Walked Between the Towers by Mordicai Gerstein

Bud, Not Buddy by Christopher Paul Curtis

Joseph Had a Little Overcoat by Simms Taback

Review your manuscript carefully, searching for hooks you can emphasize to editors. Pay special attention to features in the following categories:

- Subject matter: Do you have a "high interest" or "hot" topic?

- Setting: Does your story take place in an interesting time period or unusual place?

- Characters: Are your animal characters a popular type of animal, your humans based on beloved "types"?

- Author/illustrator: What makes you an especially apt person to handle this topic?

one hook. But try to think of other features that make your work commercial, especially if you are writing a picture book, where the hook may be more subtle than in nonfiction books. Is the book about stepfamilies, middle children, birthdays? Does it take place on Christmas or Hanukkah or during World War II? Take stock of all the features of your story and try to play up the most engaging of them in presenting your manuscript for publication.

In addition to your talent and your manuscript, a publisher will be looking for your professionalism. Professionalism has several aspects, beginning with your approach to your craft. You should appear to know language and how to use it. You are presenting yourself as a wordsmith. From your query letter on, every word you send the editor should be correctly spelled and used. Double-check your punctuation. Re-read each e-mail before clicking on "send." You should also demonstrate a professional attitude by taking a businesslike approach in communications with your editor. At the outset, be pleasant but not familiar. When criticism is offered, try not to be emotional in your response — your editor is trying to improve your story, not attacking you personally. If you feel that you cannot respond to comments without getting angry or upset, ask for a little time to digest the criticism, then respond in writing if you do not trust yourself to speak in a measured way. If you feel that your intent or expression is being misunderstood, try to explain yourself in a rational manner, and by all means stick to your guns if anyone suggests changes with which you do not agree. But be cool in

The following books all have the spark of life that makes a book irresistible to editors and readers alike. Study the authors' characterizations, dialogue, and language to discern just what it is that grabs the reader.

Harry Potter and the Sorcerer's Stone by J.K. Rowling

A Series of Unfortunate Events: The Slippery Slope by Lemony Snicket

Crispin by Avi

Harriet the Spy by Louise Fitzhugh

Duck, Duck, Goose by Karen Beaumont

Clack, Clack, Moo: Cows That Type by Doreen Cronin

stating your resolution. No one likes to deal
with a prima donna — and no one
gets to be a prima donna unless
they've already been published
and successful.

If you get an acceptance
and a contract, try to remember
that you are not the only
author on the editor's list. The
editor is working on a wide
variety of projects at any time
and will not appreciate your
making excessive demands on
his time and attention. On the other hand, you need to communicate when appropriate and necessary, and the occasional e-mail or phone call to keep in touch can
be pleasant. It can also stimulate a dialogue about present and future projects.
Above all, always be polite. Authors often feel slighted when promotion and
advertising are less elaborate then they had hoped or when sales are disappointing. Such responses are natural. But the situations themselves are almost never of
the editor's making. Most often, the editor will share your disappointment. Try to
resist the urge to call up and yell. You will only upset yourself and others, and you
may spoil your chances of working with that editor or publisher in the
future.

SELF-EDITING LIST

- Check that you have a distinctive approach to your topic.
- Analyze your writing to see that it is "alive."
- Do you show what your characters feel rather than merely tell what they do?
- Is your dialogue individual and in character?
- Does your text sound good when read aloud?
- Make sure that your plot is a logical, interesting sequence of events.
- Verify the presence of two or three hooks you can push in selling the manuscript to editors.
- Make a list of people you know who have some connection to the publishing world. Contact these people as appropriate.
- Edit your correspondence to editors for tone and content; be polite, businesslike, and thorough, but succinct.

Chapter 10

SUCCESS STORIES

"*I*f only I could get my books published!"

Writers are often so intent on that goal that they forget that publication is only the birth of a book, the beginning of its life.

After you have done your best to create a book that satisfies you, and it has been accepted by a publisher, your book's fate, either a long life or a quick, unhappy death, is in the hands of others.

And then, of course, there is the child, your reader and the ultimate judge of your book. If a child does not like a book, it doesn't matter what all of those other people think, say, or do. In the immortal words of Paul Hazard, "What precocious skill they [the children] have for skipping paragraphs, pages, whole chapters... We always hesitate, we men, to throw a book in the wastebasket because it bores us... Our habits are formed and we are so resigned that it seems as though a little boredom is necessary to real admiration. So we keep on courageously, waiting for the consoling page, even reproaching ourselves for our yawns. But the children are ruthless... they cannot be made to believe that a book which displeases them should please them...." (*Books, Children and Men*, Paul Hazard.)

Throughout this book, we have presented case histories, true stories of how real-life authors and illustrators have faced problems and solved them. We believe seeing for yourself how others did what you want to do is by far the best way to learn your craft. With this in mind, we asked well-known writers and illustrators to write short essays about how they first came to be published, and we have invited editors, agents, reviewers, book-sellers, librarians and teachers to tell you what they look for when choosing books. We are thrilled with the response and think you will be, too.

MIKE ARTELL'S TALENT BLOSSOMS IN PETITE ROUGE

Mike Artell

STARTING OUT

Mike Artell writes and illustrates children's books and teacher resource books. For two years, he also hosted his own Saturday morning cartooning show on WWL-TV (CBS) in New Orleans. Mike's books have been widely acclaimed by Publishers Weekly, American Bookseller, Working Mother *and other major publications.*

His latest book, Petite Rouge — A Cajun Red Riding Hood, *the winner of the 2004 Louisiana Young Reader's Choice Award, has been nominated for the 2005 North Carolina Children's Book Award. It was also ranked fifth on the American Booksellers Association's 2002 list of the top 76 books for kids, named a Notable Children's Trade Book by the National Society for the Social Studies & the Children's Book Council, and was recognized as a 2002 Honor Book by* Storytelling World Magazine.

An early version of Petite Rouge *was written by Mike Artell in 1991. In 1993, Mike created an audiotape of the story and in 1995 he added a simple, printed copy of the story with line art illustrations. In 1999, Dial Books for Young Children acquired the story and, after several re-writes, the current version of* Petite Rouge *was published with artwork by Jim Harris.*

I started out as a class clown. Actually, I also ended up as a class clown. In between, I was a computer salesman who, on a whim, sent a batch of terribly drawn, incredibly corny cartoons to a computer trade journal. Fortunately, the editors of that publication were looking for ways to "soften" the bland-looking pages of technical text and decided cartoons were a good way to do it. They bought nine of the ten cartoons I sent them and I was on my way to a new career.

Encouraged by my early success with the trade journals, I branched out into more general magazines and eventually into greeting cards. I created cards for a number of companies, but I had particular success with a small greeting card company in the Dallas area that also had a children's-book publishing division. One day, the art director from the children's-book division saw some of the work I had done for the greeting-card division of their company. She contacted me and asked if I'd like to illustrate a children's book. Naturally, I said yes and got my first assignment as a book illustrator.

After I illustrated the book, I mentioned to the art director that I had some children's-book ideas of my own. She referred me to the editorial people who agreed to look at my ideas. They liked what they saw and, after several meetings and phone calls, agreed to publish six picture books I had written and illustrated. Since then, I've written and illustrated more than two dozen children's books and teacher resource books.

If it sounds like the process was quick and easy, let me assure you it wasn't. Although I created my first magazine cartoons in 1977, it wasn't until 1987 that I felt I had enough momentum to quit my job and began writing and illustrating full time. Even then, it took four years for my first books to hit the market.

I don't think I would have gotten to this point without years of experience in sales and marketing. As a former businessman, I realized that publishing is a business and that publishers generally accept or reject your work based on whether or not they think they can make money selling it. I know that sounds cold, but if you think about it, it's the reason any business accepts or rejects a new product.

Does that discourage you? Don't let it. It doesn't mean your primary focus can't still be on creating wonderful books. It just means that you have to create wonderful books that will sell. Think of it this way… if your goal is to write books, then all you have to do is write. But if you want to write books that people will pay money for, you'll have to keep your reader and your publisher in mind. Both want to receive value for their investment. The reader wants entertainment, inspiration, humor, or information. The publisher wants a reasonable profit. It's a business and you ignore that fact at your peril.

Sales and marketing experience can be very helpful, but I've found other factors be equally helpful to prospective authors. Here are a few:

Enthusiasm… When you write something great, even if it's just one great sentence, allow yourself to get excited. Give yourself credit.

Persistence… Never, never, never, never quit. Eventually you'll learn what you need to know.

Terror… Terror is a great motivator. I find nothing inspires me more than my house note, car note, and my daughter's college tuition bills.

Faith… When no one else will answer your phone calls, there's always someone who will listen.

Teacher, Storyteller Adds Author to Title

Coleen Salley

Coleen Salley taught Children's Literature at the University of New Orleans for 30 years. She is now Professor Emeritus, founder of the Coleen Salley/Bill Morris Foundation, professional story teller, and the author of the popular Epossumondas series, based on the Louisiana folk tales she heard as a child. Her latest book is Why Epossumondas Has No Hair, *the cover of which is pictured on page 107.*

I want in my children's books, be they picture books or novels, just exactly what I want in my adult books. I want to be entertained. But because I am educated, older, and world-traveled, I am not that easily entertained.

A story told in words or pictures should move me emotionally. I may smile at a character or frown or cry, but I am touched in some way. A story line may seem familiar but in this book that I am reading, it has a freshness in its presentation that makes it seem new and original.

I want characters whom I remember long after details of plot have slipped away.

I want a writer who has something to say about life and living life. The theme, like a plot, may be familiar but it is worth hearing again. I take a thought away with me after I close the book, and that thought comes back to me later, some idea worthy of remembrance.

I like books that use literary devices and qualitative language that we can quote when saying that spoken English can be as lyrical as the so-called romance languages. Children have some favorites that bore me to distraction and those they find on their own without my help.

However, when I teach children's literature to adult students, I choose to mention only those books that I find entertaining. If they're good enough for children, they should be good enough for me.

An Editor Turned Agent

Andrea Cascardi

What I Look For in Choosing Books

Andrea Cascardi was, for more than 20 years, a children's-book editor. She began her career at Houghton Mifflin Company in Boston, eventually moving to New York, where she worked in editorial positions at several major publishing houses, including Crown, Hyperion, and Knopf, where she was Associate Publishing Director for Children's Books. Among the many authors and artists with whom she worked are Faith Ringgold, Karen Hesse, and Julia Alvarez. In 2001 she became an associate with the Transatlantic Literary Agency, Canada's largest agency representing children's authors and illustrators. She currently represents a broad range of writers and artists working across all genres and age groups. Ms. Cascardi has taught in the graduate publishing program at Pace University and has reviewed books and children's media for the Boston Parents' Paper. *She holds an M.S. in Mass Communications from Boston University.*

Over the course of my more than 20 years in publishing, first as an editor and publisher, and now as an agent, one thing that has always attracted me to a work of fiction has remained constant: a strong and compelling character. I'm easy prey for an unusual voice and have a special fondness for characters who are just a little bit off-center, those whose view of the world is skewed differently from my own. But, like love at first sight, my attraction to these characters can't be sustained without something deeper. Character may be the catalyst, but without a plausible and engaging storyline, and a believable and interesting cast of supporting characters, my initial spark of interest in a book hasn't a chance of igniting into something deeper. If I'm very lucky, the book might even have a few subplots to pepper the action and an evocative sense of place. But I know I've really struck gold when I find not just a book to love but also a writer with whom I can work on many subsequent books. Ultimately, what I'm really looking for is not so much in the book but in the writer: writers whose stories go deep, deep enough that they can return to the well when called on to revise and rewrite. Writers who have equal amounts of fortitude, native talent, and passion for their work. Writers who enjoy the give-and-take that comes with the creative process of sharing their private vision for a story with others. As an agent, much is required of me as well: I must be a writer's passionate advocate to the publishing community, as well as diplomatic, patient, cheerful, and persistent. For both the writer and the agent, a sense of humor is imperative. When that first tingling thrill of a new discovery somehow turns into a lasting connection, and the right relationship is struck between writer and agent, then our shared goals carry us together into the future, where that next exciting book awaits us both.

First Publication

Emily Arnold McCully

Emily Arnold McCully is the author/illustrator of Mirette on the High Wire, *which was awarded the Caldecott Medal in 1993. Her latest book is a sequel entitled* Starring Mirette and Bellini. *Samples of her illustrations appear on page 103.*

I was encouraged to read and to draw from life from the time I was three years old. Before long it was also made clear that I must be able to support myself when I grew up. Fine art, therefore, was never a possibility, while "commercial art" was. In any case, I had a strong predilection for narrative, so most of my drawings and paintings were illustrations. I loved drama, action, and character.

I rejected art school because I had so many other interests. In college, at Brown, I studied art history, which stood me in good stead later, and also wrote and acted in plays. Now, when I create a picture book, it is like writing, casting, and performing a little play or film.

After college I took a few menial jobs with small advertising agencies. I also enrolled at Columbia for a master's degree in art history, and began taking my amateur portfolio to every company with an art director listed in the telephone book. But the response was not overwhelming. I persisted, pestering people on a regular basis, for years. My first break came when Russell Lynes, then editor of *Harper's Magazine*, asked me to do drawings for a highbrow/middle-brow article. By coincidence, the next assignment was for a cover for a Harper paperback book. But work came only fitfully until I was asked to make a series of posters for a radio station that advertised itself in subway cars. The theme was children playing. I was lucky beyond my wildest dreams, and Ellen Rudin, a new editor at Harper Children's Books, saw the poster in that week and got in touch with me. She asked me if I would be interested in illustrating a children's book.

The book was a challenge and it led to another and another and before long I was making the round of children's-book art directors with my portfolio.

Picnic, a wordless book, met with success, and I began to write children's books with greater ease. Finally, I felt that my two impulses – writing and drawing – were happily united.

When I submitted my usual line-drawing sketches for *Mirette on the High Wire*, Nanette Stevenson, the art director, suggested I "drop my line." I panicked, but knew she was right. Since then, I have been teaching myself to paint and my work is generally far more ambitious (and frustrating) than before. I have been able to integrate my passion for history by fictionalizing real persons and events in picture books for older readers.

Some years ago, *Mirette on the High Wire* was turned into a musical. The various threads of my life seemed more neatly woven than ever before.

DISTINGUISHED EDITOR

Emma D. Dryden

Emma D. Dryden was born and raised in New York City. During the summer of her junior year of college, she worked as an intern at Viking Children's Books and after her graduation from Smith College with a B.A. in English language and literature, she worked for four years in the editorial department at Random House Children's Books. She began working at Margaret K. McElderry Books in 1990 and in 1998, upon the retirement of Margaret K. McElderry, became Senior Editor of the imprint. In 1999, Emma was named Executive Editor and in 2001, she became Vice-President and Editorial Director of Margaret K. McElderry Books, which is currently an imprint of the Simon & Schuster Children's Publishing Division.

Among the many award-winning books she's edited are the New York Times *bestsellers,* Bear Snores On *and* Bear Wants More *by Karma Wilson and Jane Chapman.*

In evaluating picture book submissions, I pose several questions:

Is the story told with clarity? It's a comfortable sense of continuity, pacing, and progression in a text that will entertain and hold a child's interest.

Are the characters unique and clear? Story is something happening to someone you've been led to care about. Characters with distinct personalities should lead the story to a conclusion that is consistent with their inner dynamics.

Is the setting specific? A picture book world — be it a real or fantasy-needs to be rich enough for the reader to vividly imagine and believe when he/she sees the pictures. Only when the reader cares and likes the character and believes in the setting of the story does the story's ending matter to the reader.

Is the ending consistent with the beginning? The beginning of a story will ask directly or suggest any of the following questions: What is going to happen? Will the goal be reached? Will the problem be solved? And it's these questions that must be answered fully by the end. Adults can resolve an action or problem in their own minds after a story has ended, but a young child cannot. Objectives introduced in the beginning that are not fully accomplished or resolved by the ending result in actions that feel incomplete to young readers.

How does the story unfold? Storytelling really is the process of unfolding. Details are revealed and events occur during the unfolding process, but the goal is always in sight (even subconsciously). One way to ensure a successful unfolding is by establishing a unified link in the story — a repeated theme, pattern, or phrase. Links can also be created through the use of rhyme, repetition, and rhythm.

Does the story have the right blend of spontaneity and planning? One way to hold a child's interest is to introduce uncertainty or suspense into the story. This keeps a child guessing and wanting to turn the pages. Children are open to uncertainty, but they are also desirous of logic. What is the potential text/illustration balance? Writers must allow certain details about characters and setting to be interpreted by an illustrator. Writers must allow room for illustrators to throw new light on a text, perhaps to interpret a text in a way that the author hadn't thought of. This can be shocking at first and later it can be exhilarating!

What is the language? All children love the sounds of words and they love strange words, which is why they so often love listening to nonsense and verse. Picture-book prose should not only be simple and lucid, but should have a poetic cadence that appeals to the ear.

A BOOKSELLER KNOWS CHILDREN'S BOOKS

Cynthia G. Dike

Cynthia G. Dike is the co-owner and manager of the very successful Maple Street Children's Book Shop in New Orleans, Louisiana.

When I am buying books for my children's bookshop I look for a title that I can sell to my customers on the basis of my love for the book. If I love it then maybe my customers and their children will love it as well. If the customer and the child love it, hopefully they will want another. I want them to come back to my shop so that I can recommend another book that I love. The cycle continues.

In picture books for ages four to eight, I want the first word on the page to engage me. If I am bored as an adult, how can a four-year-old's interest be held in this day of instant and passive media entertainment? I also want the illustrations to catch my eye.

Children need books where something happens. Characters should resemble real people. They need to teach grown-ups a lesson, or overcome an obstacle, or solve a problem.

Being taught a lesson is not always fun, so you do not want to be too obvious. A good example of this is a book by Demi titled *The Empty Pot*.

I love books that are funny and can make me laugh. *Dog Breath* by Dav Pilkey is a favorite.

I love books that touch my heart. *Chicken Sunday* is one of these books.

One of the most popular areas of my shop is the truck, train, and fire-engine bookcase. Customers also want books about animals, dinosaurs, different cultures, outer space, ghost stories and the list goes on and on.

Illustration is very important. I always consider the artwork before I read the story. If it is not acceptable for some reason, I usually will not buy the book.

TEACHER TURNS NEWBERY-WINNING AUTHOR

Richard Peck

Richard Peck, formerly an English teacher, has written over 25 novels for the young people he knows so well. He has won a number of major awards, among which is the Edgar Allen Poe Award for Are You in the House Alone. *In 1998, his* A Long Way from Chicago *(cover pictured on page 110) was a National Book Award finalist, and in 2000, his* A Year Down Yonder *won the prestigious Newbery Medal. He has become one of America's most highly respected writers for young adults. His latest book for teachers and writers is* Invitations to the World.

Teaching made a writer out of me. Teaching raised that question that has to be answered before putting pen to paper: "Who are the people who might be willing to read what I might be able to write?" I found those people in my rollbook.

I quit my job one day, May 24, 1971. I turned in my tenure and went home to try to write just one novel my former students couldn't call irrelevant. After six drafts the book became *Don't Look and It Won't Hurt*, still in print a quarter century later and filmed in the 1990s as *Gas, Food, Lodging*.

Was it easier to get a first novel published in 1971? Probably not. It's never easy to begin. I believe my first novel found a publisher because it was about readers, not the author. We don't write what we know. We write what we wonder about. Now I sit at the backs of other teachers' classrooms, trying to learn about the people I hope will read the books I haven't written yet.

To me, a book for a young reader is always a step one young person takes nearer maturity. In my books, that usually involves distancing the self from the peer group in order to have that first independent thought. American young people already know how to declare their independence from their parents. They need an entire literature to encourage their liberations from their peers.

(Success Stories continues on page 113.)

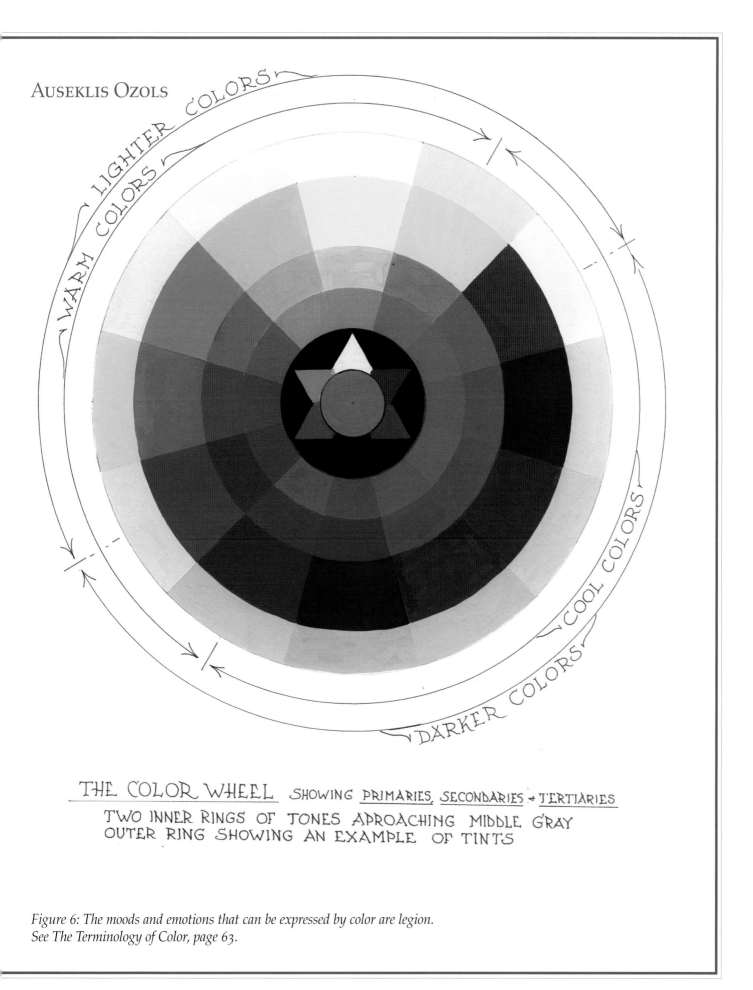

THE COLOR WHEEL SHOWING PRIMARIES, SECONDARIES + TERTIARIES
TWO INNER RINGS OF TONES APROACHING MIDDLE GRAY
OUTER RING SHOWING AN EXAMPLE OF TINTS

Figure 6: The moods and emotions that can be expressed by color are legion.
See The Terminology of Color, page 63.

Figures 7 and 8: Color and design is taught by Ozols using gouache, a water based paint. The first assignment is to design an image using only black and white (zebras pictured above). In the second lesson you may use greys (penguins pictured above). In the third lesson one more color is added; by then, the student has already learned the amazing ranges of color and design.

Figures 9 and 10: Jonah and the Whale adds two more colors to the palette, and the Partridge in a Pear Tree design shows what can be done with tones and shades. The student is not allowed to blend colors and learns the amazing ranges of color and design.

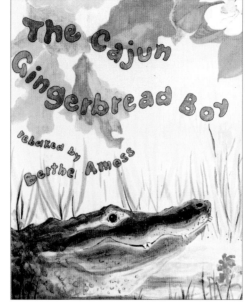

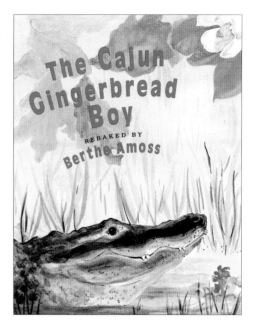

Figure 11: Berthe hand-printed the titles in letters made to look like gingerbread, but before the cover got to the printer, Ellen Friedman, the art director, changed her letters to far more legible ones in red.

Figure 12: The alligator on the original cover could be seen behind the pasted one, and the cut-off body of the alligator ended abruptly, too close to the spine.

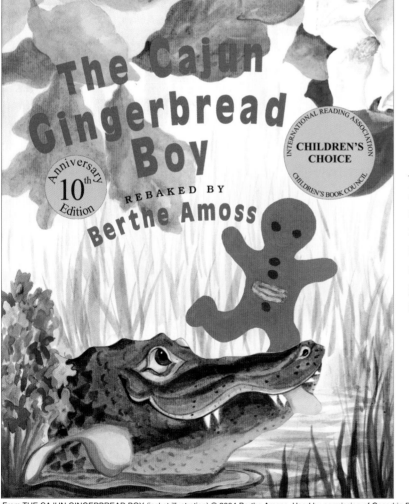

Figure 13: By the time the cover was finalized, the realistic alligator in his natural habitat, at the zoo, and in National Geographic *photos had turned into a caricature, M'sieur Cocodrie. The illustration is done in gouache on watercolor paper.* The Cajun Gingerbread Boy *is discussed on page 65.*

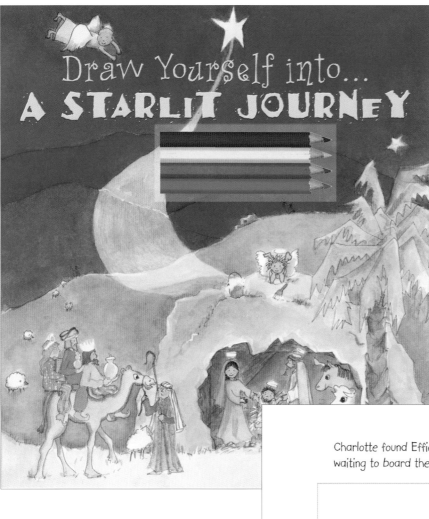

◄ *Figures 14 and 15: The* Draw Yourself Into… *books invite young readers to add their own drawing into the full color illustrated pages. Below is six-year-old Charlotte's drawing from a page in* Draw Yourself Into… the Ark.

Charlotte found Effie and drew her into the line of animals waiting to board the ark.

Figure 16: The Six Steps Workshop *grew out of the first workshops Eric and Berthe presented when they were gathering material for* Writing and Illustrating Children's Books for Publication.

In this form Six Steps *was presented for* Trial Balloons, *a children's literature program at Tulane University. It is an abbreviated version of the material in this book.*

JOAN ELIZABETH GOODMAN

Figure 17:
By transforming the girl,
Rita into the bear, Amanda,
the author made her subject at
once more "cuddly" and more
universal.

Figure 18: The artist's work is never done. Joan Elizabeth Goodman worked and reworked her pictures for **Good Night, Pippin** *throughout the submission and publication process. She sold the book to Golden on the strength of her complete book of pencil sketches. Nevertheless, after acceptance she submitted a second complete sketch dummy reflecting subtle changes in perspective, rendering and mood. The successful artist uses every opportunity to improve the book.*

Figures 19 and 20: Here we see an early color sample for the book. Note that Joan has created a picture with old-fashioned charm through the use of flat color and a placid mood. In the finished book, Joan used essentially the same composition but added richer, more modulated color and eye-catching details. The finished product is more dramatic and a better vehicle for Joan's superb storytelling.

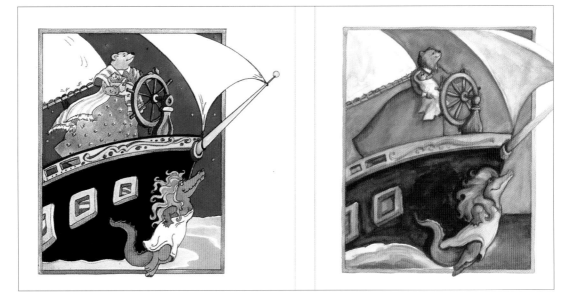

EMILY ARNOLD MCCULLY

Emily Arnold McCully's essay on getting started in publishing appears on page 93.

→

Figures 21 and 22: Shown here are illustrations from School, *a wordless book.*

→

Figure 23: The jacket from The Bobbin Girl *shows how much her style has changed.*

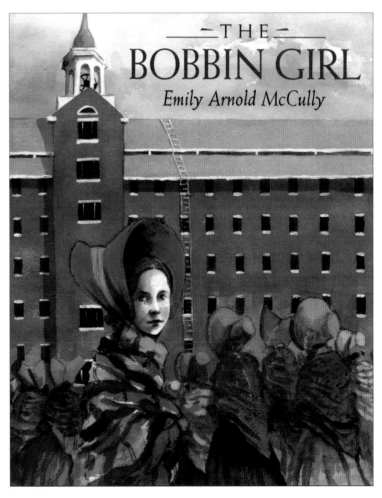

JEAN CASSELS

Figure 24: Jean Cassels' sketches are done in pencil on graphics 360, 100 per cent rag translucent paper.

Figure 25: Jean Cassels checks her thumbnail sketch for color and does a larger color sketch, then mixes her colors to begin the painting.

Figure 26: Jean Cassels' finals are done on Arches 140-lb. hot-pressed watercolor paper using gouache. She lays in large washes and goes from the general to the specific. In this book, Prairie Dogs, the last thing to do was prairie dog whiskers!

▲ *Figures 27 and 28: Jean Cassels' black and white and color sketches for*
The Mysterious Collection of Dr David Harleyson, *Walker & Co.*
2004, is the first book she has both written and illustrated.

Figure 29: Jean Cassels' final cover for The Mysterious Collection of Dr David Harleyson. The illustrations are included in the juried show, Original Art 2004, presented by The Society of Illustrators, New York, NY.

MIKE ARTELL

Figure 30: Mike Artell's award-winning Petite Rouge *ranked fifth on the American Bookseller's Association 2002 list of the top 76 books for children. You can read about Mike Artell on page 91.*

COLEEN SALLEY

Figure 31: Coleen Salley based her popular Epossumondas series on Louisiana folk tales. You can read about Coleen Salley on page 92.

CHUCK GALEY, ILLUSTRATOR/AUTHOR

Chuck Galey was born in the Mississippi Delta in a little farming town called Greenwood. He graduated from Mississippi State University in what was then called Commercial Art.

"I had everything I needed to become an artist while a youngster in the Delta," Galey says, "a pencil, a piece of paper and a long-winded Baptist preacher."

⋏ *1) I always begin an illustration with small "thumbnail" sketches. Here is a progression of ideas in which I show large bugs chasing a couple of kids who like to collect bugs.*

⋏ *2) This is a close-up development of the two characters. I've created a value sketch by shading in areas and making color notes. Small lead weights are used to help hold sketches in place.*

⋏ *3) This is a quick value sketch of the large bugs. Also, the design of the illustration continues to develop.*

⋏ *4) After transferring the line drawing to the illustration board, I've worked out a small color thumbnail drawing which will help when painting the finished art. Here, acrylic paint is used to block in some of the background color.*

5) Continuing to block in the background color, I begin to work in some of the main elements in the illustration. This work goes quickly as I've already decided on the color scheme from the small color thumbnail.

→

6) Here, detail work begins on the big bugs and the escaping children.

7) At this stage of the illustration, I've created an oil wash, a mixture of purple and green. this creates a neutral blue. When this dries, I go back in with a kneaded eraser and pull out highlights. This helps to give the illustration a cool image with depth.

9) Although the bugs are larger, the children are more intense in value and hue. Your eyes go directly to them first, then you discover the big bugs. Here, more detail is added to the children.

10) Finally, the small detail work is finished and a clean, crisp image is left to visually tell a part of the story.

8) A you can see the main characters of the illustration are beginning to show more detail. As designed in the initial sketches, I wanted the viewer's eye to first go to the fleeing children.

A LONG WAY FROM CHICAGO published with the permission of Dial Books for Young readers, a division of Penguin Putnam, Inc. 1998

RICHARD PECK

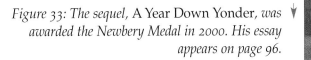

Figure 32: Former English teacher Richard Peck's novel, A Long Way from Chicago, *was a National Book Award finalist and a Newbery Honor Book in 1998.*

Figure 33: The sequel, A Year Down Yonder, *was awarded the Newbery Medal in 2000. His essay appears on page 96.*

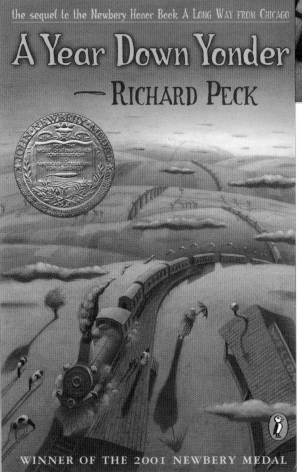

AMYE ROSENBERG

Figure 34:
Planning a book with a novelty feature takes advance planning, knowledge of the format and manufacturing process, and mastery of the special technical needs of the printer. Stickers are a relatively simple but popular "novelty" in picture books for preschoolers. In planning her Hanukkah book, Melly's Menorah, *Amye Rosenberg had to provide original color artwork, seen here, for more than fifty full-color stickers to be bound into the book.*

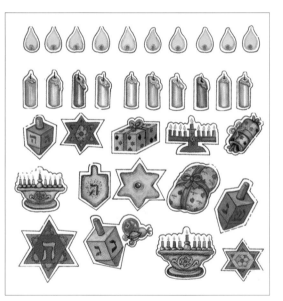

Figure 35: Amye knew that a die-cutting machine would cut around the shape of each sticker so the reader could easily peel it from the page. In order to provide a guide for the machine – a sort of mechanical cookie cutter – Amye provided a separate transparent overlay with a black ink line around each cookie sticker. She was aware that she had to leave white space around each tiny picture, so the die-cutter would not slice off any important pictorial element.

In the final book, the black line did not print. But the guide had done its job of ensuring that each sticker maintained its integrity.

Figure 36: One of the distinctive features of the book, Amye provided a picture on the back cover that children can complete as the eight days of Hanukkah progress. By peeling and placing stickers in the picture of a menorah, children can reenact the Hanukkah ritual without matches! When planning this portion of the book, Amye had to provide accurate outlines showing correct placement of the stickers.

WHITNEY STEWART

Figure 37: The jacket of Whitney Stewart's timely biography is sure to attract the attention of young people. Her story is on page 123.

NANCY WILLARD AND LEO, DIANE, AND LEE DILLON

Figure 38: Pish, Posh, Said Hieronymus Bosch, *written by Nancy Willard and illustrated by the Dillons, is discussed on page 52.*

A Reader Turned Editor

Diane Muldrow

Diane Muldrow is the Editorial Director of Golden Books, an imprint of Random House, Inc. She also worked at Scholastic, Inc. as a freelance editor and writer.

My mother tells me that when I was little, all she ever needed to do to make (or keep) me happy was to read me a storybook. Most of the books she bought for us were Golden Books. We both remember that during one particular storytime I told her that when I grew up, I would write books for children.

I've worked as an editor of children's books for 17 years, and an author for about 15. I love what I do. I think it's a wonderful thing to be able to work at something that promotes literacy, to have an actual book in your hand at the end of your labors, and to then see children on the subway or in the airport holding that very book.

Eric Suben was my first boss, actually. His enthusiasm and love for Golden Books, their history, and the talented authors and artists who created them lit a fire within me. I worked at Golden Books for seven years, and then left for another opportunity in publishing.

After some years, I was hired back at Golden Books in 1999. One of the most exciting things about the job is going into the Golden Books archives and finding treasures to bring back into print. I began a sort of "retro publishing program," and reissued lots of these titles as a subsegment of Little Golden Books, called Little Golden Book Classics. After Random House acquired us in 2001, we started up the Big Little Golden Book line — 8" x 10" hardcover versions of the classic Little Golden Books, for the library and bookstore markets. It's been so rewarding to see the classic Little Golden Books selling like hotcakes, often outselling licensed titles!

A good picture book, in my opinion, has the following elements: a colorful, bold artwork style that is not too trendy, and that will stand the test of time; and a lively story with simple, lyrical text — a crafted storytelling style, and the fewer words, the better — that contains the wonder of a child's everyday world. For us, seeing a truck drive around the corner and onto our street is not exciting; but for a child of a certain age, that truck's arrival makes him rush to the window, put his hands and nose on the glass, and stare until the truck has disappeared around the corner. A good picture book contains that wonder, that excitement.

What a Literary Agent Looks For

Jennifer Weltz

The Jean V. Naggar Literary Agency, Inc. has represented award winning and prestigious children's-book authors such as Nancy Willard throughout its 25 years. Jennifer Weltz, a partner, has been at the agency for over ten years. As well as an active client list, Jennifer sells international, audio, and film rights and manages the office and financials.

The importance of having a literary agent has grown enormously over the last ten years. A good agent will often act as an editor, and, as always, know what genre editors are looking for to fill out their lists.

As an agent I see myself as a liaison between my author and the editor and publishing house that acquires my author's work. This role takes on a myriad of forms — business manager, confidant, task master, preliminary editor, and matchmaker — to name a few. Since I take on an author's career and not just a project, I am very careful and selective about signing on new authors.

I look at all the children's-book queries sent to the agency and try to respond to all of them within a few days. If interested, I will ask for more material. If the material seems right for me and my list and right for the market's needs, I will try to connect with the author to discuss his or her vision of the book and career. Ultimately, if we seem a good fit, I will take on the author and begin submissions.

When submitting material to an agency remember to do your research!

Make sure the agency represents children's books and find out if there is a specific agent in the agency who specializes in this area. Also find out how the agency prefers submissions (queries by mail or e-mail, etc.…) For example, I prefer to receive queries by mail whenever possible.

Be sure to submit completed and polished material.

Please keep in mind that agents have many responsibilities and not a lot of time. We are always pulled by the desire to give as much time as possible to our existing authors while still keeping a lookout for new clients. Your query letter should include a synopsis of the material, information about you and any publishing history you might have. If you have a number of books you would like to show the agent, do a short paragraph for each one. If only one is truly complete, only write about that one. Remember to present careful work that is spelled correctly in a clear, legible type and include a stamped self-addressed envelope for a response.

Send your text and illustrations in their best version and package them in a mock-up.

Do not commission illustrations for your text. Publishers are always on the look-out for text to team up with illustrators they have relationships with. Send the agent the text alone in its best form for consideration.

Be prepared to make changes.

The publishing world has changed a great deal in the past few years and agents have found themselves in the role of editors more often than not. The editors rely on me to speed up their selection process by screening out unpublishable material and sending them work that fits with their current list. Consequently, when I send out material to an editor, I need to be sending out the best material possible. I usually only have one chance with each publishing house. Because of this I have been known to ask my authors for changes until I feel the material is in its best form. I always tell my authors, however, to only make changes if these changes make sense to them. This is still your work and you should never feel that you are changing something when doing so does not feel right.

When looking through queries, I look for original ideas with strong writing. One without the other is not enough. Be careful not to pick a topic that has been done over and over again. When looking at picture books, I want to be surprised, delighted, charmed…. Oftentimes I will read the book aloud since this is how it will be read when bought. I am wary of rhyme. Keeping in mind that picture books are 32 pages long with illustrations, I look for concise text that conveys a clear uncluttered story.

Lastly, remember that all agents are not alike. We have different tastes and different needs for our lists. Do not be discouraged with a rejection. Often it simply means that your material was not a good match for that agent. It is not necessarily a reflection on your work.

MEB NORTON, DISTINGUISHED LIBRARIAN TELLS HOW TO WRITE AN AWARDING-WINNING CHILDREN'S BOOK

Meb Norton

Meb Norton is Director of Libraries at Metairie Park Country Day School in Louisiana. Within the Association of Library Service to Children of the American Library Association she has served on the Caldecott Committee ("Caldecott Medal honors the artist of the most distinguished American picture book for children") and the Pura Belpré Committee ("Belpré Medals honor a Latino/Latina writer and illustrator whose works best portray, affirm, and celebrate the Latino cultural experience in an outstanding work of literature for children and youth"). She has taught Children's Literature at both University of New Orleans and Tulane University. (Quotes from the American Library Association's description of the awards.)

Not many of us know how books are selected for awards such as the Newbery and Caldecott. Meb Norton sheds light on the process.

Most awards are voted on by committees staffed with professionals who work with children's books. There is a tremendous diversity of viewpoints within the committees. Literature is so personal and subjective that it is amazing that consensus ever emerges. No one type of illustration predominates; look at the award-winners from one year and notice the wide variety of styles. Past fiction winners do show a greater number of fantasy books over other genres.

Every award from the American Library Association has definite criteria that the committee must follow. Most awards are given yearly, so a committee reads all the books that match the criteria for a given time period. Your book will be read by people who have a deep background in children's literature and who are passionate about it. Discussions are often spirited and involve serious reflection. Since there are so many books to consider, books are to be read by committee members who vote on those to be discussed by the group. Committee members are both elected by the members of the Association of Library Service to Children and appointed. They need to be members of both ALA and the ALSC division. Multi-day meetings are held twice a year for the committee to confer about the books. These meetings are confidential, as are the discussions about the literature itself. The winners are announced after the mid-winter meetings. There are winners and honor books; there is no predetermined number of winners in a category. That decision is made by the committee members. Before the public announcement of winners, committee members place conference calls to notify the author and illustrator winners. Conveying such good news is one of the highlights of serving on a committee.

Do you need to actively publicize your book? Publishers normally send copies of their list to the committee members. They generally keep up with all the criteria for each award. Committee members are dedicated to reading every book that they receive. However if you would like to submit a book, instructions are available online at:
http://www.ala.org/ala/alsc/awardsscholarships/submissioninstructions.htm

From my personal experience I have noticed that books receive an intense page-by-page scrutiny. Since there is a great deal of expertise on a committee, there is an enormous attention to detail. Science and history need to be accurate; foreign languages need to be precise. Mistakes in editing that are noticeable on the first reading are excruciating by the second rereading of a work. The illustrations definitely need to match the text on each page.

My favorite books had legs; they stayed with me over the months that we were examining books. They grew in stature during that time. Obviously a book that came out in December did not have time to build that kind of regard. Something that was new and clever and different made me stop, it grabbed my attention immediately. I would reread it several times, marveling at the book. Sometimes I realized that the book was a fleeting, manipulative attention-getter, while another book continued to delight.

A book that comes from the heart, that rings true, that you as an author or illustrator believe in has a better chance of winning an award then trying to follow a formula.

My favorite book when I was on the Caldecott committee did not even have enough votes to make it to the discussion list; however it was voted most popular book by the children of my state. It is important to remember that some of the best literature for children never won an award. Think of *Charlotte's Web*. Committees, like people, do not always have the vision to see something wonderful, memorable, and special the first time it appears in their world.

Award Winning Newspaper Art Director Turns Children's Book Creator

Kenny Harrison

Harrison is a nationally award-winning illustrator and Features Design Editor for The Times-Picayune *of New Orleans. He was part of their 1997 Pulitzer Prize-winning team for "Oceans of Trouble," the gold medal recipient for public service.*

Harrison studied painting and illustration at the School of Visual Arts in New York City. He has created illustrations for such publications as Time, The New York Times, *and* The Washington Post. *Harrison's first children's book,* How I Became Champion of the Universe, *was released by Tricycle Press in August 2002.*

I've had a love-hate relationship with children's books since I was a child. I loved the illustrations and I hated to read. In third grade I knew I wanted to be an artist. Art was the only subject in which I excelled, and besides gym, the only subject I passed.

It wasn't until I reached college that I learned I was dyslexic. I attended the School of Visual Arts in Manhattan, majoring in illustration. After a few years of freelancing with moderate success, I accepted a job as a staff illustrator at *The Times-Picayune* newspaper in New Orleans.

Being a staff artist afforded me the opportunity to hone my visual communicative skills while experimenting with many different materials and techniques in a deadline situation.

I married my longtime girlfriend one year after our arrival in the Crescent City, and our first child was born five years later. Our beautiful daughter reintroduced me to children's books. Soon I was making up bedtime stories. Four years later, our son was born and my repertoire of stories grew.

One day at lunch with co-workers I shared one of my book ideas. That was when designer and friend Beth Aguillard Straka threw down the gauntlet and challenged me to send one of my manuscripts to a publisher. I hemmed and hawed and started to rattle off my list of excuses: No time, not a writer, dyslexic — can't spell. Beth said, "NO EXCUSES, JUST USE SPELLCHECK."

We were floored when Nicholas Callaway himself called us the day he received the package. A few weeks later we flew with our spouses to New York City to meet with Callaway and his staff. The meeting went well — we returned home with a contract for three books. Our heads were spinning. We worked in our spare time, and weekends became marathons.

The Callaway staff were talented and professional. But, despite their hard work, we were unable to find a co-publisher for our project. Maybe the computer illustrations were too cold, maybe the stories were too hot, or just maybe we were ahead of our time.

By the time Callaway sent back our project, we were totally burned out. We put the books on a shelf (where they still are) and returned our attention to our families. I continued reading children's books, and on occasion I would sketch out an idea. One doodle session got me thinking. How could I write a non-violent wrestling book that would be appropriate for little kids? At first I was stumped, but I thought of one of my son's friends who was a big wrestling fan. When I made Wesley the little boy in my mind, *How I Became Champion of the Universe* seemed to write itself, and my computer illustrations found new warmth.

I made five dummies and sent them to my favorite publishers. As the rejections started coming back, I saw a cause for optimism. There was positive feedback mixed with requests for other books. One editor asked me to rewrite a couple of pages, and another wrote, "This book deserves to be published." But, ultimately, they were all still rejections.

Then, Nina Laden, a friend and one of the finest children's author/illustrators, suggested that I send a copy to Summer Laurie, a new editor at Tricycle Press. Months later, Summer called and asked, "Have you sold *Champion* yet?" It was music to my ears.

Contracts were signed and I got to work. Even though I had completed all the illustrations for the book, every page needed to be redone because the book's dimensions were larger than the dummy, and the resolution was to be much higher. Summer was an easy editor to work with. Her demeanor was warm and confident. She walked me through the entire process, and helped make *Champion* a better book.

Friends and family turned out for my first book signing. They were as relieved as I was to see a real book finally. The positive reviews and booklist recommendations were icing on the cake.

I've taken off some time from working on books, but they have a funny way of sneaking into my thoughts. Children's books and I still have a love-hate relationship, I love making them, and I hate not making them.

STARTING WITH A POP-UP

Amye Rosenberg

Amye Rosenberg is the author and/or illustrator of 70 children's books published in the United States and 17 foreign countries. These include diverse formats like pop-up, board books, anthologies and interactive sticker storybooks. Among her most popular titles are Melly's Menorah *(pictured on page 111),* Good Job, Jelly Bean, Biggest Most Beautiful Christmas Tree *and* Jewels For Josephine, *the first picture book to utilize plastic stick-on "jewels" to teach the number one hundred and the value of sharing — all in one book!*

There is a lot more to a successful career in children's books than being a dazzling author/artist, though frankly, it helps! My first publishing experience taught me that having a comprehensive understanding of different formats and a willingness to accommodate the publisher's needs is as important as being a great talent. You must be well-rounded too, willing to meet all challenges and to go where no artist has gone before!

The yearning to do a full-color picture book drew me to places where one might find a variety of material in print. One day, a friend dragged me to a gift trade show where I didn't expect to find much. I was surprised and delighted to discover a local packager of pop-up and other novelty children's books. I quickly made an appointment to visit their offices with my portfolio.

Having noticed the absence of an alphabet pop-up among their vast display, I decided to whip up a rough dummy of one consisting of sketches and even included a clumsy paper mechanical.

Their creative director was impressed with my initiative, but explained that since much of their business was foreign, all of their books had to work in at least five languages with only the black type changing. That was especially problematic with an alphabet/word format, where the words for certain objects don't always begin with the same letters in different languages.

I'd come this far and wasn't about to give up.

"What languages did you have in mind?" I asked.

Quicker than you could say *"Pat the Bunny,"* I was in the local library, tearing through French, Spanish, German, and Italian dictionaries. Suddenly I knew why I suffered through two miserable years of high-school Latin.

Word roots in the Romance language group tended to be similar, especially when referring to animals. By using international techno-terms (like telephone and automobile) and cross-referencing words and images in addition to animal characters, *Pop-up Alphabet Soup* began to take shape.

Within a week I returned with a workable solution, and *Pop-up Alphabet Soup* was on its way to publication!

However, there were more challenges ahead. Because pop-up books are multidimensional, I could not create conventional illustrations. Each spread consisted of the first page plus all the parts that would be assembled into moving elements. It was like illustrating a jigsaw puzzle in pieces. I had to work closely with their ace team of paper engineers to ensure that everything fitted together accurately and worked. Who would have thought that a book that provides the spontaneous joy of pulling tabs, lifting flaps, revealing snakes that wiggle and lions that pull peacocks out of magicians' hats, would require the precision of a Swiss watch!

The finished, printed book went to the Bologna International Children's Book Fair and was printed in four (of the five) languages. It was huge exposure for a first effort, but being a first effort, my inexperience was evident in the artwork.

I knew nothing about using my palette for reproduction (the color was too muddy or too bright) and I'd never illustrated animals before so the images were crude and inconsistent. Financially, I received little for all the effort, but it accomplished so much more.

Pop-up Alphabet Soup was a strong addition to my portfolio when I went to New York to see the "big" publishers. They were impressed with how the book evolved. It was clear I wasn't just another artist, but a problem solver who enjoyed challenge and had a thorough understanding of format, so important in children's publishing, where such a huge variety exists. This undoubtedly gave me an edge in a highly competitive industry. In no time at all, I was designing, writing, and illustrating dozens of books in dozens of different formats!

TALENT PLUS PERSEVERANCE PAY OFF

Carrel Muller Gueringer

Carrel Muller Gueringer is a writer, teacher, lower-school librarian at the Academy of the Sacred Heart, and Louisiana's Regional Advisor for the Society of Children's Book Writers and Illustrators. She teaches Writing Children's Literature at the University of New Orleans. She has written and illustrated educational activity books and has published fiction and nonfiction in magazines for adults and children. She received the National SCBWI Magazine Merit Award for her story "Thornbush" in Cricket, *February 2000.*

Perseverance is essential for a writer's success. I have met many gifted people with the talents and skills needed to write for children through my classes and through the Society of Children's Writers and Illustrators conferences. But many fail because they expect the rewards to come quickly and easily.

Writing is hard work. Skills need to be learned and improved. An understanding of the business of writing needs to be learned. These take time, and rejections can be disheartening.

Writing is lonely work. To prevent becoming discouraged and quitting, I recommend that writers join a writer's group. Education, encouragement, advice, and the support of writing friends, all these and more I have received through SCBWI.

The SCBWI is a professional international organization of people who create, produce, and promote children's literature. Membership in a professional organization indicates your willingness to go beyond being an amateur. It marks you as a person serious about your craft and your career. The benefits are numerous.

Education is one of the primary ways that SCBWI helps members. Monthly meetings give beginners opportunities to learn from others with more experience. Workshops and conferences, locally, nationally, and even internationally, provide members with opportunities to learn from and meet editors, art directors, and literary agents. The *SCBWI Bulletin*, our national newsletter, contains articles on craft, marketing, conferences, and the publishing business. Our website, www.scbwi.org, provides information on national and regional activities and the latest updates on marketing information. Through our website you can connect with and learn from a larger community of professionals.

I have met and learned from many wonderful people. I recall having Philomel editor Patricia Lee Gauch sitting in the lobby of a hotel here in New Orleans talking informally to me and other members about the qualities she looks for in a manuscript. Then, when she heard that someone was interested in illustrating, she called her art director to come down to the lobby and talk to us also. What a wonderful experience! I have found that people in the children's-book world are among the most gracious and generous. In planning SCBWI events, I have had the opportunity to call editors and extend invitations to them to meet with our group. Their responses are sometimes yes, sometimes no, but always gracious.

Professional recognition comes with membership because SCBWI teaches members the correct formatting and procedures for submitting manuscripts. Because SCBWI members send professional-quality manuscripts to appropriate publishers, some publishers will read only manuscripts from agents or SCBWI members. Beginners sometimes send fiction to publishers that only do nonfiction, or vice versa. When you meet with others who have traveled the same road, you can learn from their mistakes and make fewer of your own. Shared laughter over mistakes keeps your work in perspective and reassures you that others have stumbled along the same path.

My writing friends are my dearest friends. We share hopes and dreams, and our precious manuscripts. We critique each others' manuscripts when we meet. Their advice, their responses, and their guidance are all valuable to me. One friend climbed on top of a table and shouted, "You can't kill the mother bear!" to make her point. She was right. We are serious about our writing and take seriously each others' advice even through we do act silly sometimes. We share each others' disappointments over rejections and celebrate over each others' successes. We attend each others' book signings and bask in the glory of each others' success. We also give each other ultimatums over getting back to work on manuscripts, or just getting the manuscripts out "from under the bed" and into the mail. They won't get published if you don't send them out.

SCBWI will not find you an agent, nor will it publish your manuscript. It will make you a professional and provide you the opportunities to improve you skills and network with other professionals. You can read a book or take a class to help you along in your writing career, but the book comes to an end and the class finishes. SCBWI is always there with a helping hand.

Friendship, advice, encouragement, praise, and commiseration are all the wonderful gifts that come from a writer's group. You learn how to take advice. You will persevere, even when you have to revise the manuscript for the sixth time. Your writer friends provide the emotional support that keeps you going along the road to writing success. It is a wonderful road to travel when you have terrific people to keep you company along the way.

A Writer Turns Publisher

Aimee Garn

When I Grow Up

Aimee Garn was graduated from Mount Holyoke College and earned her MFA in Creative Writing at Columbia University. Her writing has been published in the Village Voice, *among other publications. She has long and deep connections to the publishing industry and has held responsible positions with several major houses. She is presently the president of Pretty Please Press, Inc., which published her picture books* Bella Bassett Ballerina *and* The Twitchell Sisters.

I wrote an essay in fourth grade that is now framed on my bedroom wall. Titled "When I Grow Up," it begins: "I'm going to be an Author when I grow up because I love books…The kind of books I'm going to write are going to be mysteries. And they're going to be very exiting [sic.]" I had other precocious ambitions: I was going to be a tap dancer, have a mink coat and lots of jewels, marry a millionaire, and move to Beverly Hills to meet some movie stars.

When I discovered that paper, I was around 30 years old. I was not the author of exciting mysteries, and there was not a mink coat, a jewel, a millionaire, or a movie star in sight. True, I had been the editor of my college newspaper, and I had once submitted a couple of children's-book manuscripts to an editor. But the editor had not been encouraging, and I had pursued a degree in graphic design and kept my day jobs. I had moved through a series of positions that were fine for a while, but never felt quite right; I had been a dictionary illustrator, a sales promotion designer, a product manager, and a creative director in the cosmetic and jewelry industries.

But by the time I re-read my childhood essay, by coincidence or design, I had started to write again. Without giving up my other activities, to which I eventually added becoming the mother of two girls, I wrote magazine articles, short stories, two really dreadful attempts at a first novel, a better attempt at a first novel, a screenplay, and several children's books. Along the way, I completed an MFA program in writing.

During the next 20 years I continued to write, but something was missing. Readers! I couldn't get my work published. Early on I sold a few magazine articles, but all my fiction and children's stories went, along with their rejection letters, into a filing cabinet. Two agents sent out my novel; it came back 22 times. I read books that recommended writing for The Process, not for the Goal of Publication. After two decades of Process, I thought they were full of it. Once, a children's book editor called to say that he was going to buy two of my manuscripts; his new boss later vetoed the idea. I wrote a humorous piece about my efforts, entitled "Not For Publication." I couldn't get that published, either. "Editors hate pieces about writing," a friend who taught journalism advised. "Give up."

I actually had given up, several times. Years passed; I was busy with other activities, and resigned to my failure. I chalked it up to the realities of the competitive, chain bookstore-driven marketplace, the difficulty in placing first fiction, the literary trends that did not favor my humorous work, and the vogue for celebrity children's-book authors. I doubted my ability, of course, although I had gotten enough positive reactions to feel that my work had some merit.

Still, I felt stuck and helpless. I wasn't able to join the world of published authors, and I still wanted to have my work out in the world. Then I went through what I can only describe as a Rejection Watershed — people, my community affiliations, and all those writing rejections were thrown into harsh relief. I figured out that the rejections meant that I was in the wrong place, with the wrong people. If I wanted to find acceptance, I had to push forward and past the negative experiences.

I decided to forget about selling to publishers, and try selling my work to the readers. My children's books were quirky, stylish, aimed at girls aged four to seven, which was a market I knew well. I decided to pair the books with toys or accessory items, so that together they would be a complete and unique gift. I would aim for the gift category, and identify niches where I thought my books would have appeal. Each of my first titles has a secondary market: *Bella Basset Ballerina* in the pet merchandise category and *The Twitchell Sisters*, which comes with a dress-up kit, in girls' clothing stores.

About three years ago I became the Chief Executive Officer, or the Only Officer, of Pretty Please Press, Inc. I am working alone, but have hired specialists: lawyers to investigate trademarks, to incorporate, and write my contracts; editors to check the manuscripts; illustrators; a book designer and a printing consultant, as both fields have gone through a revolution since I worked in them. My own titles debuted in winter of 2004-2005. The next two titles were books written by other authors. Again, they are books with complementary gift items and secondary markets.

The best thing about this business is that I am using all the skills and experience I acquired earlier. I am the editorial department, the art department, and the production department. I am now swinging into action as the publicity department, the sales department, and in shipping and order fulfillment. The worst thing about the business is the same as the positive: I am all the departments, functioning more easily in some areas than in others. Numbers are harder for me than words, so being the Accounting Department is not easy. I am getting help with that.

I have invested a large amount of my savings in this enterprise. At an age when many friends are retiring, I am starting a career. The jury is still out. In a few years, Pretty Please Press, Inc., purveyor of quality books for children, might be a successful entrepreneurial enterprise, or it might be known fondly as Aimee's Folly. In either case, I am finally doing what I planned to do When I Grow Up.

What a Reviewer Looks For

Susan Larson

Susan Larson is the book editor of The Times-Picayune, *New Orleans' daily paper. She has also been manager of the bookstore at the University of New Orleans and is the author of several books. She is the author of* The Booklover's Guide to New Orleans.

As book editor of *The Times-Picayune*, I see thousands of books come across my desk each year. Many are children's books to be assigned to one of our three children's book columnists. But as the mother of two eager young book lovers, I can't resist looking at them myself, and I often write about my favorites. Here are a few thoughts about working with your local press, and finding your place in the local literary community, and creating wonderful books for children.

First off, let them know you're there. Drop a line introducing yourself and your project when you move to a new place, or when your paper changes book editors. You could start by letting an editor or children's news reporter know that you've sold a book, and then remind them again before it comes out. Once your book has been published, call to be sure that it has been received, or send a copy yourself. But if you send your own book, be sure not to enclose a letter; very often, in the rush of opening many book cartons each day, accompanying paperwork becomes lost or separated. Send letters under separate cover. Make sure that you let local media know well in advance of any scheduled autographings or personal appearances for inclusion in community calendars. And read or call your newspaper to make sure you address the information to the proper individual.

Be creative in terms of off-the-book-page publicity. If your book has an unusual angle, a local connection, or a holiday tie-in, point that out. Remember that newspapers may cover library or school appearances.

Take criticism gracefully, for it is usually well meant. After all, most writers enter the reviewing world because they love books. And remember, not every book will be reviewed due to space limitations.

Find a writers' support group and attend meetings. Meet as many teachers of children's literature as you can. Make friends with librarians and booksellers. They can become powerful advocates, and remember, they are the first people who will be asked to buy your book!

Support your fellow writers by attending readings and autographings. Go to every literary festival, conference, every literary event that you can. When one writer benefits, the entire literary community benefits.

Remember that reviewing children's picture books calls for a unique set of talents, and not many reviewers are equally well versed in critical approaches to art and text. Some reviewers naturally gravitate toward color and style, and others toward a lyrical text. But most are drawn by a unique and appealing combination of word and image. It's an intensely personal and idiosyncratic reaction.

Reviews of children's books should answer several basic questions. First, I think the reviewer has a responsibility to render an opinion. Is it a good book, a bad book, a mediocre book? Is it worth the money? (As children's books become increasingly expensive, I think this is a real consideration.) Is this book by an established author/illustrator or a new one? Is the author breaking new ground? Does the author/illustrator deliver in terms of character, plot, illustration? What lessons, what values, does a child take away from this book?

My greatest asset in my work as book-review editor is that I am a reader and a lover of books. I never tire of books, and I am always looking out for something new and wonderful. And my second greatest asset is being a parent, which makes a person look at the whole world a little differently, and that includes the world of books.

I want my children to have books that are beautiful, like Bill Joyce's lovely paean to spring, *Bently and Egg*. I want them to have books that will instruct them in the sometimes sad ways of the world, like *The House That Crack Built*. I want books to demonstrate the possibilities that are open to them, like *Amazing Grace*, by Mary Hoffman, illustrated by Caroline Bunch. I want books to make them laugh, like the wonderful, witty poetry of Jack Prelutsky, which should be a part of every childhood. I want books that show the diversity and strength of families, like *Free to be a Family*, by Marlo Thomas & Friends. I look for books that will deepen the mystery of life, like Chris Van Allsburg's remarkable *The Widow's Broom*, as well as illuminate it, like Michael Bedard's wonderful book *Emily*, with lovely illustrations by Barbara Cooney, a book that gives a child's eye-view of a great American poet. I want books that celebrate the joy of reading, like Patricia Polacco's *The Bee Tree*, in which a wise grandfather describes the sweetness to be found in books. "Such things… adventure, knowledge and wisdom. But these things do not come easily: You have to pursue them. Just like we ran after the bees to find their tree, so you must also chase these things through the pages of a book!"

The very best children's books make the chase a lifelong passion.

MASTER OF BIOGRAPHIES FOR YOUNG PEOPLE

Whitney Stewart

FINDING MY NICHE

Whitney Stewart, graduate of Brown University, began writing and traveling as a teenager. On her first trip to Tibet, China, and Nepal, Stewart became enamored with Himalayan cultures. That first trip led to others, and Stewart began writing middle grade biographies and travel essays after she met and interviewed the 14th Dalai Lama, the subject of two of her books. For her next biographies, Stewart trekked with Sir Edmund Hillary in Nepal, and journeyed to Burma to interview Nobel laureate Aung San Suu Kyi. She has also published a biography of former premier of China, Deng Ziaoping.

Stewart lives with her husband and son in New Orleans, but travels often to give school and library talks and gathering material for biographies for children.

Stuck behind an elderly woman in the checkout line of a grocery store in Concord, New Hampshire, anxious to buy my boarding school, late-night-study snacks, I spotted a sign that read WRITE CHILDREN'S BOOKS. I couldn't wait to grab it. I was so impatient I forgot my popcorn, bananas, chocolate-raisin gorp and butterscotch drops. I just wanted to know how to get my stories published. This was it. I met my destiny in a grocery store. I even forgave my bad manners as I bustled past the frail old woman to snatch up the sign before anyone else stole my dream.

I was in eleventh grade, and I'd wanted to be a writer since fourth grade when my best friend, Suzy Tewksbury, and I stapled together our first book of poems on flimsy yellow paper. Hers were much better. They rhymed. And her handwriting looked like that of a writer, all swirly and pretty. Mine was scratchy and uneven. But I had passion and unbending will.

I submitted writing samples to the people who made that sign, and they accepted me. Not the writing really, but me. Their letter said I could take their course to become a children's-book writer. I didn't realize I'd have to pay money for my dream, or find time after French papers and loathsome trigonometry to write stories, but I was thrilled and relieved that someone else understood I was a writer.

I didn't finish the course. My homework alone kept me up nights. I despaired. I studied writers; their lives enflamed me. I ate up six biographies of George Sand and perfected my French. I read Proust, Hemingway, Woolf and Plath, and imitated their sentences if not their lives. A French, a Spanish, and an English teacher understood me; all three led me through literature, through biography. But publishers rejected the stories I sent.

I went on to college, learned more languages, traveled the world and got more rejection letters, the impersonal kind. Finally, a college linguistics professor guided my independent thesis on children's books. She suggested I focus on children's biography, and I turned up my nose. Too dull, I said. She persisted. I gave in. I spent the next 18 months bored by fictionalized biographies. This was the early 80s, and children's nonfiction was nothing like it is today.

Then I read Jean Fritz. Nonfiction was suddenly as alive as fiction. I couldn't get enough of her. When I'd gone through every Fritz book I could find, I wrote the author herself. And, to my excitement, she wrote me back. And what's more? She understood me, my view of nonfiction for kids. She even wrote that we were "on the same wave length as far as biographies for children are concerned." She, too, thought most children's biographies back then were "pretty dull." She said she wanted to explore human nature and so satisfy her own curiosity when she wrote biographies. Her letter struck me at a heart nerve. Fritz could never have known just how she worked on my inner puzzle.

I still didn't know yet I would write biographies. I continued to send out mediocre picture-book manuscripts while doing anything I could to be near professionals in the children's book world. I took a part-time job as a children's librarian and read my way through the collection, took summer courses on children's literature at Simmons College where I met dozens of my favorite authors, subscribed to the newsletter of the Society of Children's Book Writers, and learned editing skills working on a college publication.

After college, I became a travel agent in New Orleans so I could travel cheaply, and I begged my way into the job as publication coordinator of a travel newsletter. Finally, I published short travel pieces, but this only fed my desire to publish a book. And it had to be for children. Nothing could sway me. As a travel agent, I'd come home exhausted and out of ideas, so I wrote very little after dinner. Then I signed up for an evening course with Berthe Amoss, and I came home with new ideas. I had renewed fervor. But alas, my day job zapped me of creativity, and my stories lacked authenticity.

I was laid off from the travel agent's job (a disguised blessing, I know now), so my mother and I were free to go to Asia. This trip was the final puzzle piece.

After biking in China and eating dust for weeks, we flew to Lhasa, Tibet. I stood motionless viewing the Potala Palace where the fourteenth Dalai Lama once lived. I imagined the little monk scurrying through a thousand rooms, his worried attendants in pursuit. As I toured his residential chambers, I wiped my hand along walls hoping to touch his fingerprints that somehow remained after the Red Army invasion of the Tibetan leader's winter home. I wanted to live in Lhasa, to know the people, to belong to that rugged landscape, even if it meant having more nightmares and delusions from lack of oxygen.

With great regret, my mother and I did leave Lhasa, but we traveled on to Nepal, to the Khumbu Valley below Everest. This place too stole my mind, heart, and breath. How could I go home after the Potala and Everest? I saw myself donning maroon robes and meditating at an unknown monastery like a renegade character from *Lost Horizon*. Was I trying to escape the mania of Western life, reconnecting to a past lost except to my subtle consciousness, or experiencing the spasms of the writer's newest inspiration?

When I returned to the flat bayous and sticky air of New Orleans, I knew I needed to find my way back to the Himalayan range. As much as I delighted in Spanish moss and sweet olive, my present mind was caught on a rocky slope above the marketplace of Namche Bazaar, Nepal. I'd write about the Dalai Lama, I thought, and learn history as it happened in the highest lands of the world. Few American children would have ever heard of the Dalai Lama, and his story was a rich one I would love writing and children would love reading.

And that was that! Instead of writing a fictional picture book about Tibet, I chose to write biography. The Dalai Lama's tale was better than any I could come up with then. This idea was accepted by my first book publisher in the summer of 1987, 11 years after I submitted my first manuscript. I flew off to Dharamsala, India, moved in with a Tibetan refugee family, and interviewed the warm and wise Dalai Lama in his modest home in exile. This interview was the first of many, and it launched my career as a biographer for children. As Jean Fritz taught me in her books and her letter, biography can be the vehicle by which a writer explores human nature and history, and satisfies her curiosity.